𝒯 HE other day I went into the Bureau of Motor Vehicles to have my driver's license renewed.

The man behind the counter mechanically asked me my name, address, phone number and, finally, occupation.

"I am a housewife," I said.
He paused, his pencil lingering over the blank, looked at me intently, and said, "Is that what you want on your license, lady?"
"Would you believe, Love Goddess?" I asked dryly.
In my lifetime, I have had many identities.
I have been referred to as the "Tuesday pick-up with the hole in the muffler," the "10:30 A.M. standing in the beauty shop who wears Girl Scouts anklets," and "the woman who used to work in the same building with the sister-in-law of Jonathan Winters."

Who am I?
I'm the wife of the husband no one wants to swap with.

Fawcett Crest Books
by Erma Bombeck:

"JUST WAIT TILL YOU HAVE CHILDREN OF YOUR OWN!"

I LOST EVERYTHING IN THE POST-NATAL DEPRESSION

AT WIT'S END

I Lost Everything in the Post-Natal Depression

Erma Bombeck

Illustrated by Loretta Krupinski

A FAWCETT CREST BOOK

Fawcett Publications, Inc., Greenwich, Connecticut

Contents

To BILL, who said,
"Whatya been doin' all day?"

Ironed Sheets Are a Health Hazard

Before you read this book, there are a few things you should know about me.

I consider ironed sheets a health hazard.

Children should be judged on what they are—a punishment for an early marriage.

There is no virtue in waxing your driveway.

Husbands are married for better or worse—but not for lunch.

Renaissance women were beautiful and never heard of Weight Watchers.

Mothers-in-law who wear a black armband to the wedding are expendable.

Missing a nap gives you bad skin.

Men who have a thirty-six-televised-football-games-a-week-habit should be declared legally dead and their estates probated.

For years, I have worked at being a simple, average housewife. I am ready to face the facts. I'm a loser. Excitement for me is taking a Barbie bra out of the sweeper bag. Fulfillment is realizing I am the only one in the house who can replace the toilet-tissue spindle. Adventure is seeing Tom Jones perform and throwing my hotel key at his feet (only to discover it's the key to my freezer).

Would it shock you to know that as an average housewife I have never been invited to an aspirin lecture? You know the commercial I'm talking about. There's this ratio-balanced roomful of people sitting around finding out everything they've always wanted to know about aspirin but were afraid to ask.

"Can I drive a car after taking aspirin? Can I take aspirin with other medication? What are the ingredients of aspirin?" I worry about me. I don't want to know anything about aspirin.

After twenty-three years of marriage, you would have thought that once during that time some stranger would have called and asked me what laxative I use. My kids never tell me what the dentist said. My husband never smells his shirts and smiles. We rarely spend an evening sitting around reading the ingredients on dog-food cans. And I can't tell you when was the last time my husband offered to shampoo my hair.

I was telling my neighbor, Mayva, how commercials had evaded me and she said, "You ninny, let me see your handbag."

I opened it to reveal the usual collection of women's junk.

"That's your problem," she said. "You'll never get into a commercial traveling like that." She opened her purse. In it was a large bottle of Milk of Magnesia ("You never know when you are going to sit on a park bench with someone who needs a coating on their stomach."), a package of breath mints, a pound of Mountain Grown coffee, a hair spray, a bottle of dishwashing detergent, a compound to soak your dentures, a can of floor wax, a room deodorizer, and two rolls of (whisper) toilet paper.

"If you want to be a normal, average housewife," she said, "you've got to be ready for 'em."

Yesterday, I knocked on Mayva's door. "Guess what?" I said. "It worked. I almost got in a commercial. I was in the supermarket and I was approached by this man who wanted to know what laundry soap I used. I opened my handbag and showed him this big box. He was pleased as punch. He said, 'What would you say if I told you I'd give you *two* boxes of an inferior brand for this one?' I told him I'd say, '*You're on, Barney!*'"

"You blew it," said Mayva softly.

"I'm afraid you're right," I said.

I suppose I should be depressed, but I have a theory there are some things in this life you cannot control. It's psychological defeat. No matter what you do you cannot win.

Take my son. The other day I dropped him off at the tennis court and as his opponent walked over to introduce himself, my son froze. After the boy left, he slumped to the bench, holding his head between his knees. "Did you see him, Mom?" he asked miserably. *"He was wearing a sweat band."*

I could have cried for him. Any fool knows sweat bands always finish first. I wanted to comfort him, but in my heart, I knew the outcome. He was psychologically defeated.

I know. I was defeated for the title of Miss Eighth Grade Perfect Posture when I saw Angie Sensuous was a finalist. Angie was never carried in a fetal position. She was born sitting upright.

I knew I had blown the presidency of the Forensic League when I walked out on the stage dragging a piece of toilet tissue on my left shoe. I knew I could never shape up when I walked into the YWCA exercise class dressed in faded pedal pushers and knee-length Supp-hose when the rest of the class had leotards.

Don't ask me how you know. You just do. Your dog will never get well when you take him to the vet and all the other dogs have rhinestone collars and leashes and yours has a fifty-foot pink plastic clothesline around his neck.

You know your day is lost when you go into town and the elevator operator takes you straight to the basement budget store without asking.

You know instinctively that you will never get a hundred-dollar check cashed when the button falls off your coat. I always loved Fannie Flagg's remark that she could have won the Miss America pageant, but she got the wicker chair in the bathing suit competition. She knew.

I try, but somehow I am always the woman in the wrong line. Lines are like a foreign language. You have to know how to read and to translate them. What looks to me like a thirty-second transaction invariably ends up as a ten- or thirty-minute wait.

I am always behind the shopper at the grocery store who has stitched her coupons in the lining of her coat and wants to talk about a "strong" chicken she bought two weeks ago. The register tape also runs out just before her sub-total.

In the public rest-room, I always stand behind the teen-ager who is changing into her band uniform for a parade and doesn't emerge until she has combed the tassels on her boots, shaved her legs, and recovered her contact lens from the commode.

In the confessional, there is only one person ahead of me. A priest. Now who could be safer following a priest into the confessional? Anyone but me. My priest has just witnessed a murder, has not made his Easter duty since 1967, and wants to talk about his mixed marriage.

At my bank the other day I cruised up and down a full five minutes trying to assess the customers. There was the harried secretary with a handful of deposit slips. I'd be a fool to get behind her. At the other window was a small businessman with a canvas bag of change. I figured he had probably drained a wishing well somewhere and brought three years of pennies in to be wrapped. In the next line was an elderly gent who seemed familiar with everyone. He was obviously going to visit his money and his safety deposit box.

I slipped in behind a little tyke with no socks, dirty gym shoes, and a Smile sweatshirt. He had to be a thirty-second transaction.

The kid had not made a deposit since the first grade. He had lost his passbook. His records were not in the bank's regular accounts but were in the school section. He did not know his passbook number or his homeroom teacher's name, as she had been married near the beginning of the school year. Each of 2,017 cards of the school's enrollment had to be flipped. He deposited twenty-five cents.

He hesitated as he looked at his book, noting he had made fifteen cents in interest. He wished to withdraw it. As he was only old enough to print, he needed his mother's permission. His mother was called on the phone, which took some time, as she was drinking coffee at a neighbor's home. She said no.

He then wanted to know if he could see where they kept his money and if he could have one of the free rain bonnets they advertised. He asked directions to a drinking fountain and left—twenty-three minutes later.

I am psychologically defeated when I try to take one of those tests in a magazine to find out if I am a fit housewife and mother and I can't find a pencil in a six-room house. And when I do finally tally up my score, I discover I am not suited for marriage and motherhood, but have the aptitude and attitude for being a nun who drops out of the convent to sing and tap dance and make hit records.

Sometimes I don't know what's the matter with me. I find myself sitting around admiring weak kings. I don't seem to have the confidence that working women do. For example, the idea of taking a simple test to renew my driver's license was enough to make me drink my breakfast out of an Old Fashioned glass for a week.

I was standing in this long line at the Department of Motor Vehicles recently when I noticed the woman in front of me. She seemed just as frightened as I was. Her face was ashen, her eyes fixed, there was no pulse, and she dragged her feet like bowling balls.

I turned to the woman behind me. Either she was (a) wearing petite pantyhose that were crushing her kidneys or (b) she had just got word that her visiting mother-in-law had broken her hip and couldn't be moved for three months.

Me? I was terrified and suspicious of the whole outfit. In fact, I regard the test as a concentrated effort on the part of the Department of Motor Vehicles to get me off the road. I have taken enough tests in my time to look for the hidden words like "always" and "everybody" and "never."

Despite the fact that I had studied up on how many flares I would need to light up my tandem axle truck on an interstate highway at dusk, I was posed instead with the following questions:

"An elderly lady is crossing at an intersection against the light. Does the driver of the vehicle (a) stop suddenly to allow her to cross the street, thus snarling traffic behind him; (b) honk his horn and proceed with caution; (c) swerve and try to miss her."

I must have read that question fifty times. If I stopped, I might cause eight rear collisions behind me. Legally, I had an obligation to keep traffic moving. But if I honked the horn, the pedestrian might have a heart attack, and I would have to live with that the rest of my life. On the other hand, if I swerved, I might just pull into another line of traffic, causing an accident.

I pondered the question a full ten minutes before I asked the officer, "How old is the lady?"

"That's irrelevant," he said.

"I don't suppose you want to tell me where she is going?"

"That's also immaterial," he said.

"Does she have a son in Kansas who hasn't written her in three months?"

"What's that got to do with the question?" he asked irritably.

"Because I've just decided to run the old lady down and keep traffic moving!" I said.

The woman in the pantyhose leaned forward painfully and said, "Me too, honey."

There is absolutely nothing more horrifying to me than to go to a banquet and be separated from my husband and become a victim of the Long Banquet table. You've seen them. They're long, cold tables with 150 chairs lined on either side. Your instructions are to be seated in man-woman, man-woman style. Had I known this was going to be the case, I would have developed the body for it. Too often I have turned to the man on my left only to find him engaged in conversation with a cleavage on *his* left. As I turn to the man on my right, he too is terribly busy talking with a cleavage on *his* right. Looking across the table, I find an empty chair.

For some unexplained reason, it's always the other end of the table that's wild and raucous, with screaming laughter and a fella who plays "Holiday for Strings" on water glasses.

It's not easy having a good time by yourself. Especially if you're boring to begin with. After you eat the four

salads around you, clean your silverware, count your fillings with your tongue, clear your throat, correct the spelling of your name on your place card and clean your glasses, it's downhill all the way.

Occasionally, someone about six people down on the same side of your table will wave and you will lean forward dragging your necklace through a mound of mushrooms to wave back.

"How's Sully?" she will pantomime.

You cup your hand over your ear and shrug your shoulders to express deafness.

"How's Sully?" she repeats slowly.

"Wonderful," you shout back.

It is only after you are looking down your bra and wondering how you are going to get the mushrooms out delicately that you realize you have never heard of Sully and besides she was talking to the man sitting next to you.

Any real conversation at a long banquet table is impossible. I have discovered I can say to my dinner partner, "Did you know Ho Chi Minh wore Supp-hose?" and he will look over your head and answer, "Tell Mary. She's perfectly marvelous at faking. Never had a lesson in her life."

I cannot think of anything clever to help stamp out the long banquet table. Yet, I do not want to simplify the problem. If we are ever to survive as a nation, ever to laugh and walk free in the sun once more and help conquer mental health in this country, we must find a way.

I always wish I were one of those women who could let the phone ring and say sorta flip-like, "If it's important, they'll call back."

A friend of mine (?) actually convinced me one day that I could save hours by not answering the phone when it rang. "Try it once," she said, "And you'll never break your neck to answer the phone again." The phone rang . . . and rang . . . and rang . . . (I began to perspire) and rang . . . and rang... (I paced the floor) and rang . . . and rang . . . and then, there was silence.

"You see?" she said. "There's nothing to it. And look at all the time you saved."

As soon as she left, I called Mother. "I'm sorry I didn't answer the phone when you called, but . . . What do you mean you didn't call?"

I dialed my husband's number. "What do you want? I know I called you, but I am only returning your call, which I didn't answer when it rang. Oh, you didn't?"

Mayva's cleaning woman said Mayva had gone to town with her mother-in-law and couldn't possibly have called me.

My mother-in-law in Florida said it was sweet of me to check in, but she had not placed a call to me.

My publishers in New York said they were fine and it was always nice hearing from me but no one had contacted me that morning.

The program director of "Happy Bucks for Homemakers" said that a call to my number that morning had not been made and that the jackpot still stood at forty dollars.

The principal at the school said they had been meaning to call me, as my son had been playing in the johns again, but did not get around to it.

I called my sister to ask if she wanted me and she said . . . never mind. I phrased the question badly.

I called watch repair only to get a curt, "Madam, we did not place a call to you, nor will we until your watch is ready to be picked up."

Through conscientious dialing, I discovered my bank hadn't called, nor had my insurance man, my Avon lady, any member of the baseball car pool, or my friendly magazine salesman.

Nor did Sylvia Porter . . . the Governor of Ohio . . . Pauline Frederick, Roy Rogers, or Dinah Shore. Finally, as I was dialing in the darkness, my husband sat up in bed and shouted, "For crying out loud. Put that phone down. What would the President want with you?"

I guess what I'm saying is I fear change of any kind. Like there was always some comfort in the fact that although murder, rape, robbery, and prostitution have been on the rise in this country for some time, I could always depend on one law remaining, the tags on pillows that read, DO NOT REMOVE THIS TAG UNDER PENALTY OF LAW.

You could walk in the most elegant homes in the world, sink up to your supporters in carpet, drink coffee from bone china, and have domestics falling all over themselves, but there was always that one common denominator: a limp tag flapping under the chair like a piece of dirty underwear.

As a bride, I imagined all sorts of things would happen to you if you ripped the tag off your pillows. The IRS would fine you, Senator Joe McCarthy would put your name on a pinko list under the glass on his desk, and you would be blackballed from joining the VFW. There was some rumor that you would not bear children for seven years, but I doubted that.

One night my husband had a few drinks and threatened, "You know what I'm going to do? I'm gonna go in and rip the DO NOT REMOVE tags from the pillows on our bed." He didn't know what he was saying and a neighbor and I had to physically restrain him.

The other day I read where the Department of Labor, together with the Upholstery and Bedding Advisory Board, have reworded the tag to read,

THIS TAG NOT TO BE REMOVED EXCEPT BY CONSUMER.

Frankly, I don't know what the world is coming to. Today the pillow tags. Tomorrow, we'll be opening asparagus right side up.

Oh, I'm not lily white by any means, mind you. I've done some pretty rotten things in my life. Once, I deliberately left the cover of a matchbook open while I lit a match. Another time when I thought no one was looking I sprayed whipped cream on my strawberries without first shaking the can. In moments of anger, I've even taken the cellophane off lampshades and purposely screwed on lids in the opposite direction of the arrow.

But ripping the DO NOT REMOVE tags from pillows. That's something else. After I read the story, I went to my room and shut the door. I pulled down the spread of the bed and held the pillow in my arms. Sliding my fingers

along the seam I felt the tag. Gently, I wrapped my fingers around it and ripped it off.

At that precise moment, I heard a bolt of thunder, the cat ran under the bed and I saw small feathers oozing out of the seam where I had ripped the label.

I fell to my knees. "Bless me, Ralph Nader. I have sinned."

The world seems to be moving so fast. I know you're not going to believe this, but there has not been a how-to book on sex published in fourteen days. The little fact has made quite a difference in our Wednesday night bridge club. Last night, not one person made mention of the word sex . . . or for that matter even thought about it.

"How's your mother?" asked Maxine breaking a thirty-minute silence.

"Fine," said Mildred, "I finally seduced . . . rather induced her to go to town and check out the spring passions."

"You mean fashions," said Maxine.

"That's what I said," said Mildred. "The clothes were a drag, but we did enjoy lunch at a new place on Main Street. If you're interested, they have wonderful David Reuben sandwiches there."

We all looked silently at Mildred who stopped talking and rearranged her cards. Another half hour passed.

"An amusing thing happened to me at the supermarket yesterday," said Maxine. "I was in the express line when I realized I was down to my last sensuous . . . I mean cent."

"What did you do?" asked Mildred.

"Wrote a sex, what else?"

"You're lucky you had your sexbook with you," I said. Twenty minutes went by.

"I hope no one is on a diet," said Fern, our hostess. "I'd hate to contribute to anyone's . . . what is it they call fat people?"

"Obscene," said Mildred.

Ten minutes later, the silence was interrupted by Maxine. "Heavens, what time is it?"

"Eight-thirty," I said dryly.

"Time sure flies when you're having fun," she said.

"Well, it certainly is refreshing to sit around and talk about worthwhile things other than sex," said Mildred. "I have discovered a new dimension to me."

"Well, are we going to talk or play cards?" asked Fern. "Come on Mildred, it's your turn to bed."

"That's bid," I corrected.

"Whatya expect in fourteen days," snarled Fern, "a miracle?"

The sex thing does bug you sometimes. It used to be so simple. Now you have more manuals than a hydraulic truck. Last year, when I became old enough to buy *Cosmopolitan* without a prescription, I was intrigued by their sexy horoscopes. I would read through Aquarius, Gemini, Taurus, and Capricorn and literally blush at what was in store for them.

However, when I reached my own zodiac sign, it was always the same. "A new hair color could get you a cab. From the 10th to the 15th, it might even get you mugged (on a slow night). Stars born under your sign: Minnie Pearl, Wally Cox and Walter Hickel."

This month I opened the magazine and was thrown into shock. My sign read, "Mr. Sex and Vitality will come into your life around the second of the month."

On the morning of the second, I was quivering at what I knew would happen. Arising early, I fixed breakfast, sent the kids off to school and sat down to wait for Mr. Sex and Vitality. At ten, the doorbell rang. It was the garbage man telling me he had a rule about picking up more than five cans. I couldn't question his vitality, but how sexy can a man be who smells like cantaloupe and wilted lettuce at ten in the morning?

At eleven-thirty, as I was eating lunch, the phone rang. The voice at the other end wanted to make a house call and talk to my husband and see if we would like to spend our retirement managing a motel. He didn't sound sexy or vital, but then anyone who could get so worked up wrapping all those bathroom glasses in see-through bags . . .

That evening I stayed dressed just in case Mr. S and V rang my chimes.

"What are you dressed up for?" asked my husband. "You going bowling or something?"

"My horoscope said Mr. Sex and Vitality would enter my life today."

"That reminds me. Did you take my suit to the cleaners?"

"You wanta nibble on my ear or something?" I asked.

"Are we out of chip dip?" he asked absently.

Within minutes, he was dozing in the chair, his paper on his chest, his can of beer balancing precariously on the arm of his chair.

I wondered how Wally Cox, Minnie Pearl, and Walter Hickel made out.

I Gave Him the Best Year of My Life

People are always asking couples whose marriage has endured at least a quarter of a century for their secret for success.

Actually, it is no secret at all. I am a forgiving woman. Long ago, I forgave my husband for not being Paul Newman. Those are the breaks. I realized, being mortal, he couldn't possibly understand my dry skin, boot puddles on my waxed floor, hips that hang like saddlebags, and a house that holds for me all the excitement of a disposal plant.

How could he appreciate that my life is like a treadmill with stops at tedium, boredom, monotony, and the laundry room. That is why he comes bounding in each evening with a smile and a report of his day. Last night, for example, he munched on a stalk of celery and said, "I've had quite a day. Worked like a son of a gun this morning with Fred. Then we got in the car and toured an installation north of town. Suddenly I remembered it was

Sandy's birthday. You remember Sandy, don't you? (I remember Sandy. She was the one who burnt her bra and five engine companies showed up.) So, we treated Sandy to lunch. By the time I got back to the office, it was time to wrap up. I'm late because I stopped off at John's to see his new boat. What did you do today?"

"I fired my deodorant," I said. When he left the room I mumbled, "Paul wouldn't have been so unfeeling."

"Who's Paul?" asked my eleven-year-old.

Now, trying to explain Paul Newman's mystique to an eleven-year-old is as futile as explaining Dr. Wernher von Braun to Goldie Hawn.

"Paul Newman," I said patiently.

"The guy in *Butch Cassidy and the Sundance Kid?* He rode a neat horse in that picture."

"What horse?"

"How come you're smiling and looking funny?" he asked.

"Like what?"

"Like when you find a quarter in Daddy's chair."

"It's Paul Newman," I shrugged.

"Would you like to be married to him?"

"It has nothing to do with marriage," I said.

"You mean you'd like him to be your friend?"

"I wouldn't have phrased it quite that way."

"He's about as tall as Daddy, isn't he?"

"Daddy who?"

"Boy, ladies sure act silly over movie stars."

"I don't know if I can explain it or not," I said slowly, "but Paul Newman to a tired housewife is like finding a plate of bourbon cookies at a PTA open house. It's putting on a girdle and having it hang loose. It's having a car that you don't have to park on a hill for it to start. It's matched luggage, dishes that aren't plastic and evenings when there's something better to do than pick off your old nail polish.

"Paul Newman, lad, is not a mere mortal. He never carries out garbage, has a fever blister, yawns, blows his nose, has dirty laundry, wears pajama tops, carries a thermos, or dozes in his chair or listens to the ball game.

"He's your first pair of heels, your sophomore year, your engagement party, your first baby. Good grief, boy, he's the Eagle on its way to the moon. Don't you understand that?"

"I don't think so," he said. "Anyway, his horse was pretty neat."

As I passed the window, I saw my reflection. Flats. Head scarf. Daughter's windbreaker with 71 and two stripes on the sleeve. Mixi skirt (long and short). Who was I kidding? With the kind of day I had, I'd settle for the horse.

Like most women, I work at marriage, trying to keep alive the excitement and stimulation that made me marry in the first place. I convinced my husband that I have a friend who, every Friday, carries on a clandestine luncheon with her own husband.

She drives her car into town and he drives his. They meet at some obscure little restaurant, get a table in the rear where they hold hands and stare lovingly into one another's eyes. In the parking lot after their tryst, they kiss good-by and she whispers, "I'll try to make it next Friday."

He laughed until he snorted, "How bored can a woman get?"

"So bored she would meet Walter Brennan without his teeth . . . at McDonald's and go dutch."

"Who do you know who is that desperate?"

"Me," I said. "Every woman has to romanticize her marriage. Why don't we do it?"

"I'd feel like a fool," he said. Then, sensing my disappointment he added, "Okay, I'll meet you at Ernie's Eats next Friday."

I dressed carefully, feeling a bit foolish, yet with a

certain sense of wickedness. I parked the car and ran to him. He looked at me intently. "What are you thinking?" I asked softly.

"Did you bring your American Express card? If you didn't we'll have to go to the Beer and Bloat Palace across from the office. They cash checks on Friday."

"You devil you," I countered, "you mustn't say things like that until we're alone."

"What happened to the fender?" he said. "Another parking meter run out in front of you?"

"We do have to stop meeting like this," I said. "Every week I say I am not coming, but when Friday comes I am helpless."

"Are your corns bothering you again? You don't look too good under the eyes. Like maybe you ought to get the load off your feet."

"It's eye make-up, precious. Just for you. Notice anything else different about me?"

"You sewed the button on your coat."

"The perfume, you madcap. I won't wear it again until you promise to behave yourself."

"What'll you have?" he asked, opening the menu. "Unless you're too much in love to eat."

"Are you crazy?" I asked, grabbing the menu. "Make it two hamburgers, an order of onion rings, a double malt, and banana cream pie."

Naturally, I don't want any recognition or awards, but I've forgiven my husband for a lot of things during our twenty-three-year marriage.

1. I forgive him for not tanning. Actually, I have devoted my entire life to getting my husband tanned. I have basted him with oil, marinated him with lotions, tossed him on all sides, and broiled him to perfection. (Frankly, if I had spent as much time in the kitchen as I spent on him, I'd outdistance the Galloping Gourmet.)

It has all gone in vain. The other day I wached him inch his way out into the sunlight. He was swathed in six beach towels, a pair of dark glasses, and a pair of sandals that buckled to his knees.

"Did you lose your umbrella?" I asked dryly.

"I don't know why it bothers you that I am not tanned," he said, moving his chair to a shady spot.

"It bothers me because you don't look healthy. You look like a ninety-six-pound weakling would kick sand in your face at the beach and yell, 'Yea Sicky.'"

"When will you get it into your head that some people do not tan," he said.

"Everybody tans," I insisted. "It's just a matter of conditioning!"

"It's not a matter of conditioning."

"Doesn't it make you feel awful to go into a crowded room and have people ask, 'What happened?'"

"Look, just because I do not want to look like an escapee from an elephant burial ground . . ."

"Steve McQueen tans," I said, "and so does Paul Newman. And have you ever seen John Wayne sitting in the saddle with towels covering his arms?"

"What's that got to do with me?"

"They all look healthy. That's what it has to do. Wouldn't you like to walk down the street looking bronze and mysterious? Women would turn and say, 'Boy, does he look healthy.'"

"No."

"Just for an hour or so, let the sun do its thing. You stretch out and I'll pour three cups of oil over you and let you simmer."

From time to time I checked to make sure he was tanning evenly. Later, he came into the house and eased into his clothes.

"What did I tell you?" I laughed. "Already your clothes look better. You should see the contrast between that light shirt and your skin. And your eyes! I never knew they had color before."

Later, as we sat side by side, leafing through a magazine, I tried again. "I know you don't agree with me now, but believe me when I tell you, you are the healthiest-looking man in this doctor's office."

2. I forgive him for that performance he puts on every time he orders wine for dinner. Right away, he's Cesar Romero. First, he makes a circle with the glass under his nose. Then he tilts back his head like he is going to make Jeanne Dixon materialize. Finally, his tongue touches the wine.

The rest of us at the table sit there like idiots waiting for this man who doesn't know a vintage port from last week's Kool-Aid to decide whether or not the wine will meet with his favor or disfavor.

The waiter shifts his weight to the other foot. Finally, Cesar speaks, "A bit more please," he says extending his glass. As my eyes roll back in my head he says, "I've got to be sure."

"You have not the foggiest notion what you are doing," I accuse.

"Why would you make a statement like that?" he asks.

"Because I have that same look on my face when I squeeze melons in the supermarket and I don't have the foggiest notion what I am doing."

"For your information, my dear," he says, wiping a bit of the grape off his chin, "tasting wine is an old tradition that was once initiated to protect kings and queens from being poisoned."

"Where were you when the pot roast was served?" I ask.

As he sits there smacking his lips and wrestling with his decision, another question crosses my mind. How does the waiter know which one to have sample the wine for the rest of the group? The one with the reddest nose?

Or the one who looks like he's going to pay the check? Or the Secret Service type who goes around protecting kings and queens?

"By the way," I finally say to my husband, "you've sampled half a bottle. Do you suppose it is safe for the rest of us to have a little wine with our dinner?"

"I sent that particular bottle back," he says.

"You're kidding. Why?"

"Why indeed. You're not fooling around with some little old lady who only tipples at the faculty Christmas party. I've had wine many times before in my home. I ordered them to serve us Lake Erie, 1970, and this time I want to see cork floating around in it!"

3. I forgive him for flunking Campfire in the Boy Scouts. It's amazing how a careless camper will flip a match during a rainstorm and seconds later the entire forest will be in flames.

We will give a party and my husband will "lay a fire," using thirty pounds of paper, a mound of brittle kindling, and a seasoned log with a guarantee stapled on the side. Within minutes, an entire party will be driven into the streets by smoke.

He's the only man I know who had a fireplace with a gas lighter go out on him.

"Why don't you forget the fire tonight?" I said, collaring him before a party.

"Nonsense," he said. "I've got the secret. I just have to use more paper and get it started early. That's the secret. Start it early and get a bed of hot coals. Then, just feed it logs all night."

At 6:30 P.M., he burned the evening paper which I had not read.

At 6:40, he emptied three trash cans into the fireplace and created another small flame.

At 7:05, he emerged from the garage with a wagon

full of papers I had been saving for the last three months for the Boy Scout paper drive.

The guests began to arrive.

At 7:45, he burned all the calendars in the house, plus five napkins which he snatched from the guests.

At 7:50, he frantically tore the plastic bags off the dry cleaning in the hall closet and burned a drawerful of brown paper grocery bags I save for garbage.

At 8:05, with the living room snowing with flying fragments of soot, he began emptying shoe boxes and wedging them under the log.

At 9:00, he was reduced to lighting unpaid bills with a match and throwing them in on the smoldering log. I collared him, "Look, Smokey the Bear, will you forget about the lousy fire and pay some attention to your guests?"

"I almost got it," he said feverishly. "Just a few more pieces of paper. He ran to the cedar chest and emerged with the baby books, our wedding pictures, and our marriage license.

At 1 A.M., he grabbed me by the shoulder. "It's going," he said. "It's really blazing. Remember those cereal boxes with only a little cereal left? I threw it away and the boxes did it."

"Wonderful," I said, pulling the covers around my neck. "Now will you put it out and come to bed. We've got a big day ahead of us tomorrow. I'm going to have you committed."

Actually, my husband and I are different in many ways. Our sense of humor is different. I told an amusing story the other evening about Phyllis Diller in which an interviewer asked her if she was a neat housekeeper, like when her husband got up to go to the bathroom did she make his bed while he was gone. She replied, "Make it! I have it sold before he gets back."

My husband frowned and said, "Where would you find someone to buy a bed at that ungodly hour?" Then he retaliated by telling his dog story about the talking dog who played all the big night clubs and the talk shows. "Then one day he got sick and had to have an operation. After that, he couldn't get a job anywhere."

"How come?" asked a woman.

"Because all he did was sit there and bark."

The men howled with laughter until I thought they were going to be sick. The women sat there puzzled.

"Dear," I interrupted, "it wasn't because the dog just barked. It was because all the dog talked about was his operation."

"That's not funny," he said.

"It's not my fault," I countered. "It was your lousy joke."

"If it's my joke, then how come I can't tell it my way? Why would a dog rehash something so painful as an operation. You know what you are, you're sick. I bet if I said the dog sold his hospital bed before he got back to it, you'd have laughed yourself silly."

But being generous, I forgive him for his bad jokes and I even forgive him for being tall. I am 5'2", and he is just under 6'. According to him I get my kicks out of life by moving the car seat up to within three inches of the steering column and leaving it there.

"Okay, you win," he said, staggering into the kitchen and slumping into a chair.

"What are you talking about?"

"I am too weak to fight you anymore. My kidneys have been destroyed by a door handle. I have burns on my neck from being flogged with a shoulder belt. My head is bleeding from a clip by the mirror and I tore my pants on the left-turn signal."

"Is that what you were blowing the horn about?"

"I was blowing the horn because every time I exhaled, my belt buckle pressed against the horn."

"You are upset."

"Aren't you quick? Next year, you may even get tie shoes."

"There is no need for you to be sarcastic."

"That's easy for you to say. You have never tried to fold a pair of legs into a parachute and 'drop' into your own car before. Look at these," he shouted, putting his feet on the table under my nose. "Do you know what these are?"

"They are feet," I said softly.

"That's right. They were never meant to be folded, spindled or mutilated."

"Then why are they forked?"

"Because I have just rescued them from the jaws of the glove compartment. I thought perhaps if I crawled in from the passenger side I could wind my legs around my neck and then unwind them under the steering wheel."

"What happened?"

"I was attacked by a sun visor and in the skirmish my foot was half eaten by the glove compartment."

"I don't leave the seat up on purpose," I began.

He jumped from his chair. "Oh, but you do. You have never really gotten over not marrying the Hunchback of Notre Dame, have you? Now, *he* could have fit in your mini-car, couldn't he? You'd like one of those cardboard cars whipping around with Barbie and Ken and Midge. Or Eddie Arcaro. You should have married a jockey. Or Mickey Rooney. What a twosome you would have made sitting on your pillows! Or Dick Cavett. Storing a picnic basket under your feet. Or what about that guy on top of the wedding cake?"

I think one of the real tests of a stable marriage is being married to a man who worships at the shrine of burnt food—the back-yard chef.

Last spring, we decided to remodel our kitchen. We installed a stove that does everything but burp us, a refrigerator-freezer that coughs ice and defrosts itself, a line of counter appliances that makes humans obsolete, a dishwasher and disposer that eliminates leftovers, and shelves and storage to stagger the imagination.

On the day it was completed, my husband stood in the middle of this culinary carpetland, nodded his approval, then hit for the back yard, where he proceeded to cook our meal in a fetal position over a hibachi, using a bent coat hanger for a fork and a garbage-can lid to hold the salt and pepper.

Most men go through it. It is called the Back Yard Bicarbonate Syndrome, better known to most Americans as the "cookout."

The condition is usually brought about by the acquisition of a new grill, a fun apron that reads, BURNED IS BEAUTIFUL or a neighbor who delights and amazes his guests every weekend with dishes from his new Neanderthal Cookbook.

Somehow you cannot help but admire the courage of these virgin cooks who heretofore thought a pinch of rosemary was something you did when your wife wasn't looking and who considered aspic a ski resort in Colorado.

The big question is how to survive it.

When you are invited to a cookout be sure to check the invitation. If it reads "7 P.M." assume that is the time of arrival. The time you are served may vary as much as forty-eight to seventy-two hours from then depending on:

(a) a confused host who puts the potatoes in the oven and turns on the clothes dryer for 60 minutes;

(b) an emergency visit from the local fire department that got a call that a tire factory is burning;

(c) a group of guests who are all members of the U. S. Olympic Drinking Team and are celebrating their victory over the Russians.

In order to survive a cookout you must also be aware of some of the old myths and clichés.

There's the perennial, "After all, what can you do to a good steak?" This line is often accompanied by a high, shrill laugh and a nudge.

The implication is that it takes very little skill to throw a good chunk of beef on the grill and get it off while still edible.

The answer to this question is obviously, "You can burn it."

Secondly, no cookout is complete without a large, furry dog who hangs around the grill all night. There is a myth that large, furry dogs never take the meat off the grill and run. Unless you have chased a dog through three back yards, a shopping center, and a sprinkler you might be lulled into believing this.

Next, there is the myth about "the couple that cooks together stays married together."

The other night I tripped over my husband who was hunched over his hibachi. "Is that you?" I whispered in the darkness.

"Who did you think it was?" he asked.

"I didn't care. If you hadn't moved I was going to eat you."

"Just a little longer," he said. "Are the guests getting hungry?"

"I think so. They are sitting around watching their stomachs bloat."

"It hasn't been that long."

"Are you kidding? It's the first time I've ever seen my fingernails grow."

"Just a few minutes and the coals will be ready."

"Do you mean to say you haven't even put the meat on yet?"

"Give them some more hors d'oeuvres."

"It's no use. They're beginning to get ugly."

"Then go check everyone and find out how many want their steaks—rare, medium rare, medium, medium well, and well done."

I left and returned in a few minutes.

"Well?" he asked.

"Thirteen raws. Hold the horns."

"Very funny," he said. "How about the fourteenth guest?"

"He ate his coaster and said that would hold him."

"That tears it," he said. "That's the last time I waste my special barbecue sauce on this group of ingrates."

The survival of the cookoutee hangs solely, however, on how well he is prepared for the outing. Guests should

never be without their Survival Kit which should be stocked
with:

A flashlight to see what you are not eating.

Bright trinkets and beads to barter with the natives
for bits of food before dinner is served.

A calendar to keep track of time.

Sterile face masks to keep from getting high on bug
spray.

Dry matches for the host when he admits he was never
a Boy Scout.

The other night, after the guests had gone and I was
crawling through the grass, retrieving my silverware, my
husband said proudly, "Well, it couldn't have been a
complete disaster. Evelyn Weard just called and asked
for my recipe for barbecue sauce."

I could hardly wait until morning to call Evelyn. "Is it
true?" I asked. "Did you really ask for my husband's
barbecue-sauce recipe?"

"I certainly did," she said excitedly. "You see, the other
night when I dropped a bit of the sauce on my skirt, it
didn't spot. In fact, it took a spot out. I made a batch
of it this morning and would you believe it, your husband is a genius. His barbecue sauce kills crab grass,
took a wad of chewing gum off the dog, the oil stains
off the garage floor, and cleans chrome."

"Wonderful," I said. "Just keep it out of the reach of
children."

"I know," she said.

My husband and I have produced three children, survived three wars, comforted one another at funerals, and
dedicated ourselves to one another through sickness and
in health. The other day, I backed out of the driveway,
turned too sharply, and hit the side of his car. He was
a perfect stranger.

"Where are you going?" I asked as he left his dented fender and bolted toward the house.

"Don't move your car," he said. "I'm going to call the police."

"The police!" I shouted. "For crying out loud, I'm your wife."

"This is no time for nepotism," he said stiffly.

I should have known better than to compete with a man and his car. For years, psychologists have been telling us that a man's relationship with his automobile supersedes even sex.

For you women who are skeptics, let me ask you a few questions.

Does your husband have an insurance policy on you that includes no-fault, comprehensive, and is fifty-dollar deductible? Or do you have the basic ninety-six-dollar burial policy that puts you on a public bus and takes you to the edge of town?

Do you have a guarantee for a complete oil change every six months and/or 1,000 miles, whichever comes first? Or do you only visit a doctor's office for major surgery?

Does your husband fly into a rage if he finds someone stuck a candy wrapper in your pocket or a piece of bubble gum on your instrument panel?

Has your husband ever patted you on your trunk and remarked what a beautiful trade-in you'd make?

Does he take you to a restaurant three times a week and instruct the waitress to "Fill her up"?

Does he care if the kids put their feet on your upholstery?

Does he object if your teen-agers drive you all over town?

Would he pay eight dollars to have you towed anywhere?

If you didn't start in the morning, would he stay home from work?

If you answered "No" to any or all of these questions, then you have a four-wheel corespondent in your divorce suit.

As the policeman surveyed our situation, he turned to my husband and said, "Sir, you are illegally parked. Your car should be at least fifteen feet from the edge of the driveway. Are there any witnesses to this accident?"

"Just my wife," said my husband smiling at me.

"I never saw this bum before in my life," I said.

After the policeman had gone my husband mumbled, "Joanne wouldn't have been so unfeeling."

"Who's Joanne?" asked our eleven-year-old.

"Joanne Woodward," said my husband. "I don't know if you'll understand this or not, son, but Joanne Woodward is like shaving at twelve, she's like going to buy a car and having the salesman take you directly to the convertibles. She's like having your mother-in-law allergic to you, and not having to have a belt to hold your suitcase closed.

"Joanne isn't mortal. She never wears hair rollers, never has chenille marks on her face, and never cleans a fireplace without gloves. She doesn't have to stand up to lose her stomach or talk about worming the dog during dinner. Joanne is. . . ."

"Does she ride a horse good?" asked his son.

"I knew you were too young to understand," he said sadly. "But I forgive you and I forgive your mother."

Talk to Me—I'm Your Mother

For the first two years of a child's life you try to get him to talk. For the next ten years you devote your life to getting him to shut up. For the remainder of his life you try to get his lips moving again and sound coming from his throat.

Personally, I have always said if the Good Lord had meant for me to speak in the mornings, He'd have put a recording in my chest and a string in the back of my neck.

I don't understand people who can hop out of bed and synchronize their lips with words to form sentences and communicate ideas. I don't reach this point until after lunch.

I have a basic morning vocabulary of twenty words: "No. I don't care. It's in the dirty-clothes hamper. What's your name? Mustard or catsup? In your father's billfold." There have been no subtractions or additions in twenty-three years.

The other morning I shuffled to the kitchen and me-

chanically did my thing. My daughter said, "I need to buy. . . ."

"In your father's billfold," I interrupted.

"Where's my favorite V-neck sweater?" said a son.

"In the dirty-clothes hamper."

"Can I wear it?"

"No."

"Then I'll sit by an open window and probably die before lunch."

"Mustard or catsup?" I muttered, holding his sandwich.

"Catsup."

As I opened the sandwich and tried to force the catsup out, the phone rang.

"Hello," said my daughter. "Just a minute. It's for you, Mom."

I shook my head.

"She can't come to the phone now," she said tartly. "She's hitting the bottle."

"What's your name?" I asked my youngest. He told me and I scribbled it on his lunch bag.

"Wilma Whiplash called," said my daughter, pressing a message in my bathrobe pocket. "She'd like to meet you for lunch at the House of Chicken."

I nodded. And all morning I thought about Wilma Whiplash. Who was she? Had I met her and couldn't remember? Was she an old schoolmate? An Avon lady? A program chairman? An editor's wife? One of my children's teachers? A secretary trying to peddle underground pictures of the office Christmas party?

"I'm Wilma Whiplash," said a voice at 1 P.M. at the House of Chicken. "I know you don't know me, but I read your column in the newspaper and figured you'd be a scream at lunch."

"What's your name?" I asked dryly.

"Wilma Whiplash," she smiled. "Your dress is darling. Where did you get it?"

"In the dirty-clothes hamper."

"Ah . . . what are you drinking?"

"I don't care. Mustard or catsup."

"Where do you get all your wild ideas?"

"In your father's billfold," I said numbly.

I felt sorry for her, but it served her right.

Communication has always been a problem among families. We started off with one child who was misunderstood literally. From the day he uttered his first word to present day, no one seems to know what he is talking about.

For some unknown reason, I am the only one in the family who can translate. When he was a toddler, he stood for hours at his father's elbow, shouting, "Me no, na, noo noo," and his father would shrug and say, "What does he want?"

"Well, what do you think he wants?" I'd say irritably.

"He's either telling us the dog hates cold spaghetti, he hates the encyclopedia we bought for him, or he just swallowed his pacifier."

"He is trying to tell you he dropped a cookie down his drawers. I mean how dense can a father be?"

As he got older, things got worse.

"That kid has to have his mouth fixed," said my husband.

"What now?"

"He just told me he has to know all of his bowels by tomorrow because the teacher is having an English elimination."

"He's always had troubles with v's," I said.

"That isn't all he has trouble with. If he goes around talking like that, they're going to put him in a class where he makes recipe holders out of wooden blocks and clothespins all day."

"All he's ever tried to do," I sighed, "is imitate the rest of the family and he doesn't know how to pronounce the words yet."

"I'll say," said his brother. "He told the whole bus the other morning that you were a syndicated Communist."

"And he told everyone his teacher had hubcaps put on her teeth so they would look better," said his sister.

"And he told a client of mine on the phone the other night that I couldn't come to the phone because I was unapproachable. Really, something has to be done. At a football game the other night he yelled out, 'All we need now is one perversion and we win the game.'"

"What's the matter with that?" I snapped. "I told him myself one player had a mucilage separation in his shoulder and another was having trouble with his nymph gland and with the quarterback having a sensuous shoulder, we needed all the perversions we could get!"

You should have seen my family sit up and look at me. I guess it's because I don't lose my temper too often.

Then we have the other extreme of a son who speaks only four words a year. One day as I was separating an egg, the whole thing cracked and slithered to the floor. He looked at me and said, "Way to go, Mom."

My eyes misted. I didn't think he even knew who I was.

I have always been envious of the mothers of children who talk. What an insight they must have into the personality of their child. What good times they must enjoy . . . the intimate laughter . . . the first blush of a shared secret.

Our relationship is a lot like the President and Congress.

"What's that hanging out of your notebook?"

(Shrug shoulders)

"You're having your school pictures taken tomorrow? And what's this one? An insurance form for football? I didn't know you went out for football. What do you play? *When* do you play?"

(Grimace)

"Hey, here's one directed to my attention. They need someone to bake cakes for the ox roast. I think I could manage that."

"That's left over from last year."

"Oh, here's one. 'Memo to: Revolutionary Troops. Cross Potomac tonight at 7:30 P.M. Bring money. Signed George Washington.' Thought I'd toss in a little humor there."

(Sigh)

"Look here. You're having an Open House. I think I'll go."

(Moan)

Now, if you think things at home are painful for the

mother of a non-verbal child, you should try enduring Open House.

No sooner was I in the door than a mother accosted me and asked, "What do you think about Miss Barbie and Mr. Ken in the boiler room? I'm sure your son told you about it, didn't he?"

Then another one approached and said, "I would have known Mr. Brickle just from my son's description, wouldn't you?" (Lady, I wouldn't have found the building if there hadn't been a Boy Scout in the parking lot.)

Finally, "It's a shame you were too busy to come to the Booster's Awards. We thought since your son was on the team. . . ."

As I was ready to make my exit, my son's teacher put a hand on my arm. "I want to talk about your son's problem," she said.

So! It wasn't me. It was definitely a case of a poor, shy boy who couldn't express himself, so he lived in a world of silence.

"Your son can't seem to keep his mouth shut," she said. "He talks incessantly during class, shouts out the answers before there are questions, and is known to his classmates as 'Elastic Mouth.' "

"He's never been what you would call a talker," I confessed. "At home he talks in bulletins. Like the people on television where a husband says to his wife, 'Cold gone?' and she nods and replies, 'Fever's down. Cough disappeared. Feel great!' I mean when he comes home from school, I feel like Ironside interrogating a witness."

It's true. I always try to initiate a conversation by asking, "What kind of a day did you have at school?"

"Bummer."

"There are some doughnuts in the bread box if you want them."

"Dig it."

"Your brother took a bite out of one, but. . . ."

"Gross."

"Who was that boy I saw you walking with?"

"Hard man."

"You like him?"

"No."

"You don't like him. Why not?"

"Comes on strong."

We were having one of our exciting exchanges one night when his father came in.

"Will you listen to him?" I shouted. "If this boy doesn't start communicating, we're going to have to give him injections to keep his throat from drying up."

"He's no Buckley," shrugged his father.

"Are you kidding? I tried lying in the middle of the floor when he came home from school one afternoon just to see if the sight of my lying there unconscious would generate conversation. Know what he did? He leaned over my still body and asked, 'Did *Sports Illustrated* come?' "

"You are going to have to bridge the gap," said my son's teacher. "Cross over into his world and show him you care."

A few weeks later, I broke one of my own house rules. I entered his bedroom. (We were going to wait until he got married and then sell the house.)

He had a notebook before him and was picking his teeth with a ballpoint pen. "What's the greatest threat to man's environment?" he asked suddenly.

"This bedroom," I said, looking around in disbelief.

"People," he amended. "They're careless, and I am writing a paper on how we can help."

"Where do you keep your bed?" I asked, bustling around.

"In the middle of the floor," he said. "It isn't made because I am airing it."

"You've been airing it for three years," I said. "Why have you been sleeping with forty-eight copies of *Sports Illustrated,* a Dixie cup, a hubcap, and eighteen mismated socks?"

"Ecology is a personal thing," he mused. "It has to start with one person at a time. Every candy wrapper is important. Every bottle cap."

"Why are my eyes watering?" I gasped.

"It's the aquarium," he said. "The catfish just isn't doing his job."

I looked at the polluted bowl of water with the pump that gasped and gurgled. Other than the Cuyahoga River in Cleveland, it was possibly the only body of water to catch fire.

"Carelessness," he continued. "I think that's what it is all about. If you could just make people aware of how they are cluttering up our countryside."

"Are you saving those soft-drink bottles for anything?" I asked.

"There's a garter snake in one of them," he said off-hand. "Now, where was I? Oh yes, clutter. How about, 'We must all band together and form groups to bring pressures against the Earth Molesters.' How's that?"

"Wonderful," I said. "Did you know you have gym shoes under your bed that have rusted? A three years' supply of crumpled nose tissue in your sock drawer? A piece of green bread under your pillow? A pre-schooler under your clothes on your chair? A nest in your toothbrush and a towel on the floor of your closet that just spoke to me?"

"Mom," he said. "are you gonna help me with this paper on ecology or talk?"

I guess what it boils down to is that I don't trust anyone under thirty. I didn't trust anyone under thirty when I was under thirty. Particularly, I don't trust children. It isn't that they mean to lie, it's just that by omission or fancy mouthwork they spin some of the most incredible stories since Jack London.

One friend of mine was asked by her son one day whether he could go on a chartered bus to New York to see a basketball game.

The request seemed reasonable. She asked all the usual questions. "Was it chaperoned? Were there others going? Was it a school function?"

She didn't find out until about fifty-five irate parents called her that her sixteen-year-old, newly licensed son was driving the bus into New York City. He failed to mention that small detail.

With teen-agers particularly, you have to touch all bases. You have to learn to speak and translate obscurity.

"May I go to a party Saturday night?" she will ask.

"Who is giving it?" asks the parent.

"One of the girls." (Your own daughter)

"At a house?"

"Yes." (Yours)

"Are the parents going to be there?"

"Probably." (Providing the parents can drive from Miami, Florida, to Cleveland, Ohio, in three hours)

"Who else?"

"Just some of the kids from school." (There are five schools in the entire district)

"How many?"

"Twenty or thirty." (Couples)

"I assume it will break up early."

"Definitely." (With a little help from the local police)

I could write an entire book on the incredible stories my children pass on to me as gospel. One told me about a boy he met at camp who was closely related to Howard Hughes. However (here comes the zinger), since Hughes had disappeared he didn't get his allowance, and for twenty-five cents he would swallow a fly. My son believed him.

On another occasion he told me of a classmate (seventh grade) who flew his own airplane and was hijacked to Minneapolis one weekend. My son believed him.

He approached me in the kitchen one day and asked, "What day is it?"

"Tuesday," I said. "Yesterday was Monday and tomorrow is Wednesday."

He cocked his head to one side and asked, "Are you sure?"

They say communication at the dinner hour is the most important part of child rearing. When our table began to sound like F. Lee Bailey's summation, we decided to do something about it.

"We are both at fault," I said to my husband. "Why don't we knock off picking at the kids while we eat. No chewing around about bicycles left outside to rust.

"No nagging about how they have the table manners of a weak king.

"No confrontations about report cards, dirty rooms, or bringing home the car with the tank empty.

"No harping about the garbage stacked up on the back porch, whose turn it is to do dishes, and who has the scissors in their room. We've got to stop criticizing them while they eat or they're going to have ulcers."

At dinner that night things were painfully silent.

"We had an amusing speaker at Kiwanis today," said my husband, "who spoke on nuclear survival."

The kids chewed in silence.

"You'll never guess who I met in the Cereal and Spices aisle today." They ate stiffly, only occasionally exchanging glances with one another.

"Anyone notice I defrosted the refrigerator?" I asked.

"Hey, has anyone heard what a five-year-old child said

to Art Linkletter when he asked what animal she wanted to be when she grew up?"

Finally, one of the children spoke.. "Don't you wanta know who broke the storm-door windows?"

"No dear, eat your dinner," I smiled happily.

"Aren't we going to talk about who left the lids off the garbage cans and the dogs got into them?" asked another.

"Absolutely not," said my husband. "This is no time to discuss unpleasantries."

"Aren't we even going to talk about who traded who on what night and whose turn it is to clear?"

"Not during a meal," I said softly.

As if on cue, all of them pushed themselves away from their half-eaten dinner.

"What's the matter?" I asked.

"We can't eat when you're sore at us," they said.

Getting through to kids is not easy for parents. Especially when they go into their "locked door" syndrome. Our entire house used to be open range. Anyone could graze anywhere and still be in plain sight. Now it has all the charm of a mental institution.

The other night I knocked loudly on the bedroom door.

"Who is it?" asked a voice.

"It's Mama."

"Who?"

"Mama!"

"Are you sure?"

"Yes."

"What do you want?"

"Open the door. I want to talk to you."

"Did 'he' send you to get his records back?"

"No. Unlock this door."

The door opened a crack and one eye peeked out. "Oh, it's you."

"You were expecting Donnie Osmond? Come to dinner." The door slammed shut.

Following a telephone wire, I traced the next child to a locked closet.

"I know you are in there. The telephone wire is warm. Come to dinner."

There was silence. Then a whispered voice said, "She's listening. I'll call you back."

The next one was a toughie. I found him behind a locked door in the garage playing his drums.

"Do you hear me?" I shouted. "It's dinner."

"Who told you I was here?"

"The neighbors."

"Is that all you want?"

At dinner I asked them, "Why do you feel you have to lock yourselves in your rooms? Surely, we can respect one another's privacy without bolts and chains. Getting this group to a dinner table is like cracking the First National Bank."

"Look, Mom," they explained patiently, "we are going through a phase of our lives when we need privacy. We have to have time to find ourselves . . . to find out who we are, what we are, and where we are going. Surely you can understand that."

Later that evening, I had locked myself in the bathroom, when a note slid under the door. It read, "I need a quarter. Where is your purse?"

I wrote back, "I am finding myself. If I don't know who I am, it's a lead pipe cinch I don't know where my purse is."

The experts say there is a time to talk and a time to be still. With teen-agers you're never quite sure. I was riding with my daughter when suddenly, for no reason, she turned down a dead-end street. Cautiously I said, "You'd better turn around." She kept going so I raised my voice and said, "There is a guard-rail approaching us and I think you'd better turn around." She sat there frozen to the wheel until I finally shouted hysterically, "For God's sake, *stop*."

She slammed on her brakes, turned to me, and said softly, "Can't we ever talk? You're always shouting at me."

Now that might not sound like a formal invitation to you, but to me it was like a Bird of Happiness chirping. "I've wanted to talk with you for a long time," I confided, "particularly about selecting a college. I've been noticing that you've been getting application blanks from schools behind the Iron Curtain and thought you might like a little help from Daddy and me in choosing a school."

"Why should you want to visit a campus?" she charged. "You're not going there."

"Indulge us," I smiled. "We are old people and we are high-strung. Your father and I just want to make sure there are alligator-stocked moats between the girls' and boys' dormitories and that the dorm mothers aren't smoking funny cigarettes."

"I wouldn't mind it if you just look," she sulked, "but you and Daddy will ask a million questions like, 'How much does it cost?' and 'How many ironing boards are there on each floor?' and 'How many students are there in each class?' Dumb stuff."

The first school we toured we liked. Academically, it was tops. She shook her head hopelessly. "That's easy for you to say. Did you see those five boys in the Student Union? Short. Short. Short. Short. Short."

The next school we visited also had some merit. (Also five ironing boards per twenty-five girls.)

"You're kidding," she said. "The ski slopes are a day away."

The third one had a poster of Fidel Castro in the administration building, but other than that it seemed acceptable.

"No way," she complained. "The registrar had a burr haircut."

Other schools met with disfavor because (a) a chaplain made you write to your mother once a month; (b) their football team had a bad season; (c) Pauline Frack had been accepted and if they took Pauline Frack they'd take anybody!

"I wish you'd be more like Wyckies' mom and dad," she said. "They check out campuses but they don't bug anyone."

My husband and I had never toured a campus tennis court by flashlight, before, but at least our daughter was talking to us. She said, "Crouch a little more."

Her departure for school was quite dramatic. Not that she spoke a lot, but her actions moved us to tears.

As my husband and I walked through the gutted, bare rooms of our home, our footsteps echoed hollowly on the bare floors. Finally, my husband spoke, "It's incredible, isn't it? It took us twenty-three long, married years to amass eight rooms of furniture, forty-three appliances, linens for five beds and an acceptable wardrobe, and now . . . it's all gone."

I nodded. "And to think she condensed it all in two large suitcases and a zippered gym bag."

"I just don't believe it," he said, closing the doors on the bare linen closet. "The sheets, the towels, our electric blanket. All gone. Why don't you make us a cup of coffee?"

"Can you drink it out of an ashtray?"

"Forget it," he said, "I'm going to sit down and. . . ."

"I wouldn't," I cautioned. "She took that small occasional chair you used to sit in."

"And the TV?" he gasped.

"The first to be packed. Along with the transitor radio,

the hair dryer, the make-up mirror, the electric skillet, your shaver, and your parka jacket."

"And I suppose the phonograph is. . . ."

I nodded. "College bound, along with the typewriter, the electric fan, the space heater, bulletin board, label maker, bowling ball, popcorn popper, and full set of encyclopedias."

"How will she lug all that stuff back to school?"

"I think she dismembered the bicycle and put it under her seat."

"What are we going to do?" he asked, looking at the barren rooms.

"If we looked better we might get on 'Newlywed Game' and try to win a washer and dryer."

"I think we've got enough Green Stamps for . . ."

"Forget the Green Stamps," I said softly. "She took them."

"We could take a trip and. . . ."

"If we still had luggage," I corrected.

"This is ridiculous," he snarled. "Why can't she go to school right here at home?"

"She wants to get away from our materialism," I said.

One Size Fits All of What?

SHAPE UP OR SING AS A GROUP

The women in the Mortgage Manor housing development just started a Watch Your Weight group. We get together every Monday for coffee and doughnuts and sit around and watch each other grow. Somehow, it makes us all feel better to know there are other women in the world who cannot cross their legs in hot weather.

The other Monday after I had just confessed to eating half a pillowcase of Halloween candy (I still have a shoebox of chocolate bars in the freezer to go), we got to talking about motivation of diets.

"When my nightgown binds me, I'll go on a diet," said one.

"Not me," said another. "When someone compliments me on my A-line dress and it isn't A-line, I'll know."

"I have to be going someplace," said another woman. "I know as sure as I'm sitting here if someone invited

me to the White House I could lose fifteen pounds just like that!" (Snapping her fingers)

"I am motivated by vacation," said another one. "I starve myself before a vacation so a bunch of strangers who have never seen me before can load me up with food so that when I return home I look exactly like I did before I started to diet."

"Home movies do it for me," said a woman, reaching for a doughnut.

"You mean when you see yourself and you look fat in them?"

"I mean when they drape me with a sheet and show them on my backside."

Finally, I spoke up. "There is only one thing that motivates me to lose weight. That is one word from my husband. My overeating is his fault. If he'd just show annoyance or disgust or say to me, 'Shape up or sing as a group,' I'd do something about it. I told him the other night. I said, 'It's a shame your wife is walking around with fifteen or twenty excess pounds. If things keep going on I won't be able to sit on a wicker chair. What are you going to do about it?' I asked, 'just sit there and offer me another cookie? Laugh at me. Shame me into it! Humiliate me at parties!' Sure, I'd get sore, but I'd get over it and I'd be a far better, thinner person for it. Just one word from him and I'd be motivated!"

"Diet," he said quietly from behind his paper.

"Fortunately, that wasn't the word. Pass me another doughnut, Maxine."

WEIGHING IN

I have dieted continuously for the last two decades and lost a total of 758 pounds. By all calculations, I should be hanging from a charm bracelet.

Although I kid Weight Watchers a lot, it is the only organization in which I ever lost a great deal of weight. But I fought them.

Every Thursday morning, a group of us had to "weigh in" before the lecture. Our ritual was enough to boggle the imagination. We got together a checklist of precautions before we actually stepped on the scale.

Bathroom? Check. Water pill? Check. Have you removed underwear, wedding rings, nail polish? Check. Set aside shoes, corn pads and earrings? Check. Are you wearing a summer dress beneath your winter coat? Check.

The first week I stepped on the scale and my instructor said, "You have gained." (Next week I cut my hair.)

The next week, she said, "You have lost eight ounces, but that is not enough." (I had the fillings in my teeth removed.)

The third week, I had dropped a pound, but my instructor was still not pleased. (I had my tonsils taken out.)

Finally, she really chewed me out. She accused me of not sticking to the diet and not taking it seriously. That hurt.

"I didn't want to tell you," I said, "but I think I am pregnant."

"How far?" she said coldly, clicking her ballpoint pen to make a notation on my card.

"Possibly three days," I said.

She glowered, "Any other excuses?"

"Would you believe I have a cold and my head is swollen?"

"No."

"How about I was celebrating the Buzzard's return to Hinkley, Ohio, and had butter on my popcorn?"

She tapped her pen impatiently on the card and stared at me silently.

"Lint in the navel?" I offered feebly.

"How about first one at the trough?" she asked dryly.

I learned quickly never to argue with a woman who had the scales on her side.

I saw my old instructor the other day and she eyed me carefully and asked, "When are you returning to class?"

"As soon as I have my appendix removed," I said, returning her gaze.

I'm not sure, but I think I heard her moan.

THINK FAT!

I am sick and tired of people saying to me, "Boy, do you have it made. A sober husband, three healthy kids, a house in the suburbs, and a little part-time job to keep you in pantyhose."

Well, let me tell you, my life is not all pretzels and beer. How would you like to get up every morning of your life and confront a seventeen-year-old daughter who is 5'6", weighs 110 pounds, refuses to eat breakfast, and insists, "I'm not hungry."

Every time she says it, it burns me up. I set two alarm clocks to make sure I don't miss a meal, and she says, "I'm not hungry."

My husband says I am suffering from repressed antagonistic rivalry that manifests itself in many strained mother-daughter relationships and simply means resentment, jealousy, and competition between us.

"Nonsense," I told him. "It's just heartburn from the cold cabbage rolls I ate before I went to bed last night."

The other morning as I forced down three pieces of bacon she left untouched, I had it out with her.

"Look," I said, "it's not normal to wake up in the morning and not be hungry. From the time you eat dinner the night before to the time you eat your lunch at school, it is sixteen hours. That's too long between meals."

"But some people don't need food."

"Don't need food!" I gasped. "I don't want to frighten you, but a buzzard followed you to school the other morning."

"I can't help it. It upsets my stomach when I eat."

"Do you know what you are doing to your mother?"

I sighed. "Killing her. That's right. I don't know how much longer I can go on carrying you. When you were a baby I didn't mind eating your leftovers . . . the strained peas, the mashed squash, and the puréed lamb, but as you got older, the burden became greater. Having two breakfasts for the last seventeen years is beginning to show on me. I put on weight easily. Remember when I got a flu shot and put on three pounds from it? But, if you don't care what happens to your mother. . . ."

"The dog doesn't eat his breakfast and you don't yell at him," she said, slamming out the door.

You know something? With a little catsup, it didn't taste bad.

FATTIES VERSUS THINNIES

If there is one person in this world I have absolutely no compassion for, it's a size five telling me she'd like to put on weight and can't.

It's like Zsa Zsa Gabor complaining to a spinster that they don't make drip-dry wedding dresses.

One of these frails nailed me in the supermarket the other day and charged, "Why don't you ever write about thin girls who are just as miserable being thin as fat people are being overweight?"

"Look, thermometer hips," I said, looking around nervously, "if the girls in TOPS see me talking to you I'll be dropped from their (excuse the expression) rolls. You're a no no."

"But why?" she whined. "How can we have peace in the world when fatties and thinnies can't communicate?"

I looked up tiredly. "What do you want from me?"

"Tell me how you put on weight," she said.

"This is ridiculous," I sighed. "I don't know how I do it. All I know is I gain weight when I have to eat my own words. I gain weight when I chew on a pencil. I added five pounds in the labor room."

"You must have some tips you can pass on to thin girls on how to gain weight."

"All right, here is the BOMBECK FLAB PLAN."

1. Go on a diet. There is no better way to gain weight than to call up everyone you know and tell them you are going to lose fifteen pounds by the time the pool opens on Memorial Day. You can sometimes add as much as two pounds a week.

2. Agree to go to your class reunion. As if on cue, your waistbands will grow tighter, your chins will cascade down your chest and you'll grow shoulders like Joan Crawford.

3. Read a cookbook before retiring. Rich recipes at bedtime are hard to digest and tend to turn to fat. They also tend to get you up in the middle of the night to fry doughnuts and make malts.

4. Sit next to stout people. Overweights are contagious. They always carry food on their body and have an overwhelming urge to share it. I have gained more weight in exercise classes, health spas, and centers than anywhere else.

5. Drastic measures: Get pregnant. Suffer a hangover (at least your head gets fat). Look into the new fat transplants. I have this chubby friend who is such a willing donor . . . in fact, I'll even throw in my Debbie Drake record.

YOU WANT ME FOR LUNCH?

In trying to rationalize my flab the other day it occurred to me that the high cost of dieting is keeping me portly.

Think about it. Did you ever see a fat Ford sister? Or an obese Rockefeller socialite? Or a tubby in the White

House? Face it. The good life begets a slender figure. The truth is they can well afford the dietary food products, the fresh fruits out of season, the imported fresh fish and the lean steaks.

They can absorb the cost of new wardrobes and extensive alterations to the old ones. But mostly, they can go the health and spa routes which cost anywhere from $2 to $1,500 a pound.

Actually, I have seen only one plush spa in my life. It was the Elizabeth Arden spa in Phoenix. A friend of mine was spending a week there and called me and said, "We'd like to have you for lunch."

"You are desperate for roughage, aren't you?" I said.

"I mean we'd like to have you as a guest," she said.

It's a beautiful, incredible place. To begin with, it is lousy with mirrors. (I had the good sense to take all mine down when I passed a mirror one day, sucked in my stomach, and nothing moved.)

All the dietees wear white terry-cloth robes and scuffs and wonderful smelling cream on their faces. They are massaged, pampered, exercised, sunned, and rested on a schedule that is carried around in their white terry-cloth pockets.

The lunch was simple. Cottage cheese, fresh fruit, and Ry-Krisp.

"I wish I could afford not to eat like this," I said sadly, "but I come from a home where gravy is a beverage."

"Don't be ridiculous," said my friend. "You could duplicate the spa in your own home . . . schedule and all."

At home, I slipped into my chenille duster with the button over the stomach missing and consulted my schedule in the pocket. At 8 A.M., I ate the leftovers from breakfast. At 9 A.M., I sat on the washer during spin which did wonders for my hips but dissolved my breakfast. At 10, I chinned myself fifty times on the guard rail of the bunk beds. At 11 A.M., I jogged to the garbage can, followed by luncheon at noon (cottage cheese) and beauty treatment at 12:30. (I rubbed hand cream on my elbows.)

I lasted until 1 P.M. By this time my bathrobe was hot and the cottage cheese had worn off. Then I saw it. A half of an Oreo cookie in the carpet. I leaned over and popped it into my mouth and smiled my fat little smile. Money may make you thin, but you cannot buy ecstasy.

THREE SIZES FITS ALL

I have always admired women who can wear a one-size swimsuit. That is, either a size 12, a 14, or a 16. I wear all three sizes at the same time.

In the modern-day vernacular, I can't seem to get it all together. My friends tell me exercise is the secret. It's not how much weight you carry, it is how it is packaged and distributed.

I stood in front of the mirror the other morning and assessed myself. Imagine if you will the state of Texas. I look terrific at Amarillo, but by the time I hit Dallas and Fort Worth, I begin to blouse, and don't really thin out again until Corpus Christi. (But after Houston, who hangs on to see Corpus Christi?)

I've exercised. I really have. Once I signed up for a course at the neighborhood YWCA. The classes were held in a church and because of the popularity of the class, we were put in the church proper. One afternoon the minister visited and paused long enough to see me in a pair of pedal pushers trying to touch my nose to my bent knee which was resting on a pew and said, "You are desecrating the altar." I transferred to cake-decorating class and licked my way to six additional pounds.

For a while I used to eat my dessert at breakfast while watching a Swedish girl on television. She held me spellbound by winding her leg around her neck. I watched and listened to her for over a year and one day I wheezed, strained and gasped and finally got one of my ankles hooked over the other. I quit before I really hurt myself.

The idea of going to a spa really intrigued me. I thought how great it would be to splash around in the water and steam your pores and ride a bicycle to nowhere, but going to a spa is like having a cleaning lady. You can't go to a spa looking like you need to go to a spa any more than you can have a cleaning woman walk into a house that needs cleaning. Somehow, I just couldn't get myself in shape for a towel.

For the last year, I have watched my husband faithfully execute his Air Force exercises (which could account for the decline in enlistments). If there is anything in this world more boring than a man who exercises regularly, I have not met it.

"You should join me," he keeps insisting. "A few push-ups; a little jogging. It's good for the old body."

"Then why aren't your knees straight when you bend over to touch your toes?"

"I suppose you could do it better?"

"Sure, by letting my fingernails grow fourteen inches."

He's not fooling around with some amateur.

WRINKLE CITY

All I said was my face was beginning to look more like John Wayne's every day of my life.

Then my neighbor said she had this book on body and facial exercises that you can do while you do your housework.

And the next thing you know, I got a box of homemade cookies from my bread man's wife. I don't understand it.

I guess it started the first day I began to exercise. I was on the phone, talking to my neighbor with my knees partially bent, my legs apart and as I talked, I slapped my thighs together. When the bread man walked by the window, I waved. He waved feebly, put a package of brown 'n serve rolls on the milk box and left.

Later that week in front of the picture window, I rolled my head slowly five times from left to right, then five times right to left. In between I would shake my head from side to side going faster and faster until everything was a blur. I thought I saw my bread man running toward his truck.

For my neckline, I was instructed to stick my tongue out as far as I could and try to curl the tip. As I did so, I noticed my bread man looking back at me with both his fingers in his ears and his tongue extended. He looked ridiculous.

The following week I worked on my chin, by throwing my head back and biting into an imaginary apple with my lower lip protruding. I could really feel the chin and neck muscles pull and tried to tell my bread man so, but he stood at his truck, folded a coffee cake like a newspaper, and literally threw it into the bushes. That was strange.

I didn't see him again for a week. By this time, I had worked up to the face lift exercise. As I did the breakfast dishes, I winked with my left eye and at the same time lifted the side of my mouth. As I winked and smiled, winked and smiled, I looked up to see the bread man staring at me.

That was the last time I saw him.

His wife called and thanked me tearfully for being the single guiding force that cured her husband's drinking problem. That same afternoon, I found a box of cookies in my mailbox from her.

Yesterday, my neighbor came over with a new guide to beauty. She said for tired brains, just sit in a chair with arms loose at your sides and pretend you're floating on a white cloud in the blue sky.

Like I told her, "With crazy people running around like my bread man, I'm afraid to close my eyes."

CREEPING UNDERWEAR

We have virtually erased bad breath in this country, stamped out dandruff, and done away with burning, itchy feet, but we have been unable to conquer one of society's most dreaded diseases: Creeping Underwear.

Everyone talks about Creeping Underwear, but no one does anything about it. Technical research has put powdered orange juice on the moon, yet on earth we are still plagued with pantyhose that won't stay up, slips that won't stay down and girdles that should contain a WARNING, WEAR AT YOUR OWN RISK label.

To suggest that Creeping Underwear changes a person's personality is the understatement of this decade. The other night I went to a movie, a fully confident, well-adjusted, stable, human being.

Two hours later, I was a totally different person. My slip had crept to my waistline to form a solid innertube which added about fifteen pounds to my form.

My girdle, in a series of slow maneuvers, had reached several plateaus during the evening. First, it slid to my waist. Upon finding this area was already occupied by a slip, it moved upward, cutting my chest in half and gradually moved upward to where it pinched my neck and caused my head to grow two inches taller.

The pantyhose were quite another story. They kept

sliding down until I realized halfway through the movie that I was sitting on the label in the waistband and that if I dared stand up the crotch would bind my ankles together.

I tried to adjust these garments in a way so as not to call attention, but every time I bent my elbow, two straps slid onto my shoulder and bound my arms like a strait jacket.

My husband was the first to notice the change in my personality. "What are you doing sitting under the seat in a fetal position?" he asked. "Are you trying to tell me you do not like the movie?"

"I am suffering from Creeping Underwear," I whispered.

"You should have taken a couple of aspirin before you left the house," he snarled. "Now, get up here and sit up straight in your seat."

He didn't understand. They rarely do. Nearly 98.2 per cent of all the victims of Creeping Underwear are women. As I sat there I looked under the seat next to me and saw another woman in a similar position. "What are you doing down here?" I asked.

"I crossed my leg and was all but flogged to death by a loose supporter," she sighed.

"Do you think they'll ever find a cure?" I asked hopelessly.

"I hope so," she said. "Your tongue is beginning to swell."

GOOD-BY, GIRDLE

This generation must be doing something right. I read in the paper last week where a girdle factory shut down from lack of sales.

I regard the obituary of a girdle factory with mixed emotion. It's like having your mother-in-law move out because you have snakes in your basement. There is something good to be said for girdles. Maybe I'll remember what it is.

The problem with girdles is that they are designed under the law of redistribution. They really don't contain the flab; they merely reappropriate it. For example, when I put on a girdle, three things happen immediately: my stomach goes flat, my chin doubles and my knees inflate. So I always say, "What does it profiteth a woman to have a flat stomach if her teeth become loose?"

I have had some miserable experiences with girdles. One was with a miracle garment that I bought while carrying one of the children. It was expensive and rather complicated and came with some rather explicit instructions.

It read, "Welcome to the Constrictor 747. The Constrictor 747 is mechanically engineered to take inches off your waist and hips. When laced and hooked properly it will perform for 18 hours without adjustment. Before wearing, please familiarize yourself with the two pressure exits located over each kidney. In the unlikely event oxygen is required, the stays will open and automatically eject an oxygen mask. Please extinguish all fire material and place the mask over your face and mouth and breathe normally."

The Constrictor 747 was a great disappointment to me. I was wearing it one afternoon when a friend saw me and asked, "When is your baby due?"

"I had it two years ago," I said, and went home to give the Constrictor 747 a decent burial.

After that, I stuck with a little cheapie . . . a model called the Little Nothing Tourniquet. It was reinforced over the tummy, the hips, the rib cage, the legs, the seat, and sometimes the ankle. But it did the job. You may have seen it. When I started wearing shorter skirts, everybody saw it. It cut me just above the knees. One day my daughter said, "Gee, Mom, haven't you heard? This is the era where you let it all hang out."

And that, my friend, is what is closing girdle factories.

BOOTS! BOOTS!

I have no idea of the circumference of my legs. I only know they are bigger than a water glass, smaller than a furnace duct, and impossible to fit into the knee-length boots.

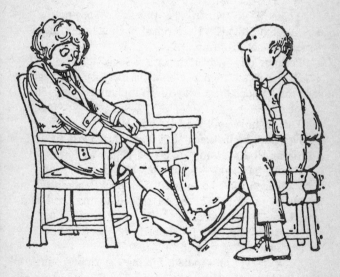

It is probably my own sensitivity, but I always imagine boot salesmen are the lowest in seniority. They are serving time in this department only because their father, who owns the store, wants to keep them humble.

My salesman was a leg watcher. (Not mine, however.)

"I would like a pair of boots," I said.

He scrutinized me closely, squinted his eyes, and appeared with a pair of Arctic boots that laced up to the knee.

"No, you don't understand," I said, "I don't want to get a construction job. I want a pair of dressy boots to wear with wools and jumpers."

With detachment, he went over to a display table and returned with a boot so long and narrow it had an echo. There was only one pair of legs in the world that would fit into that boot: Phyllis Diller's. (As a friend of mine once remarked, on Phyllis's legs, "The last time I saw legs that size they had a message attached to them.")

"Where's the zipper?" I asked.

"There is no zipper," he yawned. "They're the new easy-stretch pullons." He reached in to take out the tissue paper and got his arm stuck.

"Perhaps one with a zipper," I suggested.

He placed the zippered boot on my foot and began to ease the zipper all the way up to my ankle bone. Then it stopped.

"Thanks anyway," I said, "but . . ."

"No, no," he insisted. "It'll work. Just twist your foot a little and bear down." A crowd began to form.

"Really," I said, "it's no use. The boot is too. . . ."

"We can do it," he insisted. His pocket comb fell out and he ignored it. The blood rushed to his head and I feared for a nosebleed.

"Maybe if you took off those heavy hose."

"My nylons?" I gasped.

"Look, lady," he shouted, forcing the zipper, "suck in! Suck in!"

My leg throbbed. I spoke softly. "I appreciate what you are trying to do, but just bring me that pair over on the center table."

"Are you sure those are what you want?" he asked.

"They'll do fine," I said. I slipped easily into the ankle-length white boot with a stencil of Cinderella and a castle on the side. I may not be a fashion plate, but I'll be a smash at Show and Tell.

DISCRIMINATION

As a woman who thinks a needle is something you take out splinters with and step on in your bare feet, I have always been annoyed with the inequality of alterations.

Why is it when a man buys a suit, his alterations come free, but when a woman buys an outfit of equal or more value, she pays extra?

I was with my husband a few years ago when he bought a $49.95 suit (with a vest, two contrasting pairs of slacks, a matching tam, and a set of dishes). Not only was it a cheap suit (the label said, "Made in Occupied Guadalcanal: Fashion Capital of the World") but it hung on him like an ugly blind date.

"I don't like the way it breaks across the shoulders," he said, twisting before his three-way mirror. "And the sleeves—I like them short enough to count my fingers. Maybe you can reset them."

"No problem," smiled the salesman.

"There's too much slack in the seat and the waistband seems a little loose . . . maybe a tuck or two."

"Of course," grinned the salesman. "Let me summon a tailor."

The tailor spent thirty-five minutes chalking up my husband's anatomy. The suit looked like a steer being divided for two freezers—all at no charge.

The other day I tried on a dress of comparable value.

"It bags a little in front," I said, looking sideways into the mirror.

"There are operations to correct that, honey," she yawned. "Or we'll alter it for three dollars."

"And the sleeves. They hang so long."

"That'll be two-fifty or you can roll 'em up and keep your elbows bent."

"I don't know," I pondered. "Maybe a knit isn't for me. It clings so."

"Tell you what," she said, "if you want to save two dollars, just block it yourself by stretching it over a chair for a couple of days . . . or a sofa depending on how loose you want it."

"How much to shorten it?"

"Four dollars," she said, "but it'll be worth it. This dress will look like it's been made for you. Here, let me help you with the zipper."

"How much for helping me with my zipper," I chided.

"I'll throw it in," she said. "I feel sorry for you."

PAJAMA TRYOUTS IN BOSTON

I knew when I got a pair of "at home" pajamas for Christmas, I could never wear them "at home." They were definitely not apparel to unclog a sink, paper-train a dog, or make pizza in.

They were pajamas to sit on the sofa and cough in. Or descend a stairway with a brandy snifter in your hand. Or pose for a magazine ad which read, "Erma Bombeck could afford any oven she wanted, but she chose a Kenmore."

That's why I took them out of town for a trial run to get the bugs out before bringing them into my living room.

The place was a reception in Boston. I shook them out of the suitcase, belted them, and took off.

In my own mind, I envisioned my entrance as having the same impact as you would have seeing Elizabeth Taylor jog. I imagined conversation coming to a hush, glasses paralyzed in mid-air, jealous hearts taking the caps off their suicide rings and a voice booming, "You and your sexy pajamas! You have our hearts, you she-devil; must you have our souls too!"

My entrance produced as much excitement as a paper-clip display in the lobby of the bunny club.

"You're late, luv," said one of my friends putting her arm around my waist. "Good Lord, what's that?" she asked, her fingers touching a lump around my waist.

"It's my slip," I said.

"Doesn't it bother you?"

"Only when I walk. Do you like my outfit?"

"You look like someone I saw in a movie a while back."

"Bette Davis? Katharine Ross?"

"No, Dustin Hoffman. There's something wrong with your cleavage."

"What cleavage?"

"That's what I mean. You're wearing your darts backwards. You know something? I think you've got this thing on backwards. Hey gang, come look at this. Would you say the zipper goes in front? Maybe if you wore a bathrobe over it. . . ."

I think the pajamas need a little work before I bring them into my home town for their big opening.

BE YOURSELF!

I was walking along a center aisle of a department store the other day when a representative of a cosmetics firm smiled and beckoned me over to the counter.

"You mean me?" I giggled.

She nodded. Then she leaned over, sized me up and whispered, "I can help."

I was overwhelmed with the way she looked and the

way she smelled. There sure wasn't any peanut butter growing under her fingernails.

"First, dear," she said, "I want you to walk for me."

I felt like a fool. Stiffly, I swaggered out to handbags and back again. "Are you carrying your money in a knotted handkerchief tied to your knees?"

"Why? Am I walking funny?"

"A bit self-conscious perhaps," she said. "We'll work on that later. Now, we are going to create a new you. First, your shape. You can do all kinds of artificial things to change it. Don't turn your back on me, dear."

"I'm not," I said miserably.

"Oh. Well, all that can be fixed with padding. As for your hips and waist, there are cinchers to wear. Now, for the important parts. Do you do anything to your hair?"

"I put three rollers each morning on the side I slept on the night before."

"Perhaps a wig," she mused. "We'll just slip this one on for effect. Now, what about eyelashes?"

"Those fake ones make me drowsy."

"You weren't putting them on properly," she said authoritatively. "Now, we'll accent your cheek bones with a dark make-up making your face look thinner. You are rather sallow. We'll add this rouge to make you look vibrant and healthy. There now. Have you always worn glasses?"

"Only since college when I went steady with a parking meter my junior and senior years."

"I would suggest contacts. They really give the eyes a new dimension. And your nose. Are you happy with it?"

"It works O.K."

"I meant the shape of it. You know cosmetic surgery is very commonplace nowadays. You should have it bobbed and give your face a better profile. Of course you were planning to have your teeth capped."

She worked on me for over an hour. At the end of the

session, I was laden with creams, liners, rouge, powder, nutrients, fake eyelashes, wig, waist cincher, padding, and suggested doctors to cap my teeth, fix my nose, and outfit me in contact lenses.

"Thank you very much," I stammered, "you've certainly been a help."

"Just one last bit of advice, dear," she said softly, touching my shoulder. "Be yourself!"

YOU LIED, SOPHIA

The beauty secrets of the stars never worked for me. I remember once Arlene Dahl suggested placing chilled cucumbers over each eye to relieve tension. My husband leaned over to kiss me hello, thought it was Daddy Warbucks and has had a twitch in his right eye ever since.

Dolores Del Rio, an older star who remains ageless, said she retained her youth by never smiling and creating laugh lines. Any mother knows it's not the laugh lines that create valleys of facial erosion, but the crying lines.

I suppose I should never have trusted Sophia Loren when she was quoted in a magazine article as saying, "All I am I owe to spaghetti." Just by looking at her I would never have thought that. Good posture? Maybe. A new baby? Possibly. A sixteenth-of-an-inch padding? Oh, c'mon. But spaghetti!

Spaghetti being my favorite food, her advice was easy to take. At least once a week, I would get out the big pot (not me, you fool, the other one) and begin the ritual that is called "spaghetti sauce." Then I would toss up the salad, rich with oil, load the garlic bread with butter, reverently face Sophia's picture on the wall and say, "This one is for you, Sophia."

As the weeks went by, it became obvious my sand was not settling in the same proportions as Sophia. While she was built like a cut diamond, I was taking on the shape of a pyramid. But I persevered.

"Well, Sophia," jeered my husband, "how are you and Marcello Mastroianni making out?"

"I had it for lunch," I said.

"It's funny," he said, "but I cannot remember Sophia walking around with a safety pin in her slacks."

"A sex symbol cannot be built in a day," I retaliated.

It wasn't until I began to think the "before" pictures in magazines looked great, that I realized the road to beauty is not paved with spaghetti. Sophia lied to me. It was all a hoax to make the women of America look like beasts, while Sophia slithered her way through movie after movie. (Like having ugly bridesmaids so you'll look good.)

Taking off "spaghetti," my friends, is like taking off no other food. You can run around the block and take off an eclair. You can do a few sit ups, and dissolve lobster dipped in butter, but spaghetti hits your hips, takes roots and begins to grow again.

The other night as I sat nibbling on a piece of carrot, I watched Sophia in a movie with Cary Grant. I couldn't help but wonder . . . maybe if I left off the Parmesan.

Put Down Your Brother,
You Don't Know Where He's Been

My husband's idea of a fun vacation is sitting around watching a ranger pick his teeth with a match cover.

My idea of "roughing it" is when you have to have an extension for your electric blanket.

My husband is one of those idiots who leaves pieces of bacon out to attract bears to the camp site.

I once trapped a gnat in my bra and went to bed with a sick headache for a week.

"Face it," I said, "we are incompatible. I want to go to New York and see some theater and shop and you want to go to Murk Lake and watch mosquitoes hatch their larva."

He stiffened. "I am not going to New York and watch a bunch of lewdy nudies cavort around the stage."

"And I am not going to Murk Lake and watch men shave out of double boilers."

"I am not going to the city where I have to wear a necktie to bed," he continued.

"And I am not going to a camp ground where life is so primitive the animals come to watch us feed."

The point is we are incompatible on the subject of vacations.

"You don't understand," I said to my husband. "I don't ask much in this world. All I want is a few weeks where I could sleep in a bed where the alarm clock is on the opposite side.

"I want to go to the bathroom, lock the door, and know that when I look through the keyhole I will not encounter another eye.

"I want the phone to ring and have it be for me. I want to walk in a room and see all the drawers closed. I want to drink a cup of coffee while it is still hot.

"Don't you understand? I want to pick up my toothbrush and have it be dry."

He was silent for a moment. Then he said, "Why didn't you say so? We'll compromise. We'll go camping."

I know for a fact that a lot of families who travel together have a swell time. They play "Count the Cow" until they faint. They wave to "Out of State" license plates and sing gaily, "Getting to Know You" in two-part harmony. Our kids play a game called, "Get Mama." Or, "The Family That Camps Together Gets Cramps Together."

It's a 400-mile non-stop argument that begins when we leave the driveway and doesn't end until Mama threatens to self-destruct.

The players include a daddy who drives in silence, a mama who listens in silence, a daughter who keeps repeating, "Mom!" and two brothers who make Cain and Abel sound like the Everly Brothers.

Just for the mental discipline, I kept a record of the last "Get Mama" game. The kids argued for seventy-five miles on whether or not you could run a car a hundred miles in reverse without stalling. They used up fifty miles debating how workers in the U. S. Treasury Department could defraud the detectors by putting hundred-dollar bills in their mouth and not smiling until they got out of the gates.

It took them longer to resolve the capital of Missouri than it took to settle the entire territory. They argued about whether or not you could use a yo-yo on the moon. Whether hair would grow over a vaccination. Whether a gorilla if put at a typewriter could eventually produce a best seller. How come some daddies have wrinkles in their necks and others didn't. What size shoe Pete Maravich wore. And if a nun were allowed to become a priest, would you call her Father.

They threatened to "slap" 55 times, "punch" 33 times, said, "I'm telling" 138 times and whispered, "I'll give you one" three times. (That sounded ominous and I didn't turn around.)

As I sat in the front seat nervously knotting my seat belt into a rosary, I concluded our family would never make a TV series . . . unless it was "Night Gallery."

As I slumped against the door, one of my children yelled, "Hey, Mom, you better push the button down on your door or you'll fall out."

If only I could believe that.

It does not impress me one bit that every year more than a million families embark on a camping venture.

I know that of those who make it back (some poor devils wander around for years looking for ranger stations, children, and ice-cube machines) a goodly number are disenchanted. Why you may ask yourself?

To begin with, few realistic camping guides have been written. Usually, they are small, shiny booklets with waterproof covers (this should tell you something) showing a family in a small, secluded paradise. Daddy is in a trout stream up to his creel in excitement. Mother is waving nearby from a pair of water skis. And the children are gathered around a campfire playing Old Maid with Gentle Ben.

It never rains on the covers of camping guides. Mother is never shown doing a three-week laundry in a saucepan. Dad is never depicted fixing a flat on a tandem trailer in Mosquito City, with three children dancing around, chanting, "We are going to miss 'Mod Squad' and it's your fault." It is never revealed that children often sit around for four days at a time crying, "Make him stop looking at me or I am going to bust him one."

There are all kinds of camping, of course. There are the primitives who sleep on a blanket of chipmunks under the stars and exist only on wild berries and what game they are able to trap in the zippers of their sleeping bags. There are the tent enthusiasts who use cots, ice coolers, matches, transistor radios and eat store-bought bread, but who draw the line at electricity and indoor plumbing. Finally, there are the wheelsvilles. They run the gamut from the family that converts the old pickup truck to a home on wheels to those who rough it with color TV, guitars, outdoor lounge furniture, flaming patio torches, ice crushers, electric fire lighters, showers, make-up mirrors, hoods over the campfire, plastic logs, Hondas for short trips to the city, and yapping dogs that have had their teeth capped.

It doesn't matter how you camp. The point is that a few practical suggestions could keep you from going bananas:

What to do when it rains. Rearrange canned foods, plan a side trip, write letters home, remembering to lie. Read all the wonderful books you brought and promised yourself to read. *(The Red Badge of Courage* and *The American Journal on Tooth Decay.)*

And rains. Pick grains of sand out of the butter, sit in the car and pretend you're going home, find out who really has gym shoes that smell like wet possum.

And rains. Send the kids out to find traffic to play in. Call in friends and watch the clothing mildew. Pair off and find an ark.

Otherwise camping can be loads of fun. Tips from my woodland log:

How to bed down without hurting yourself or anyone else.

1. Don't kneel on the stove to let the cot down from the wall until all the burners are off.
2. If the table converts to a bed, make sure it has been cleared.
3. Whoever brought the guitar along sleeps with it.

4. If the wind is blowing southward, sleep northward of the person who bathed in mosquito repellent.

5. Place the kid who had three bottles of pop before bedtime nearest the door. Oil the zipper of his sleeping bag before retiring.

6. If you are sleeping on the ground, make it as comfortable as possible by using a rollaway bed.

7. Make sure all the cupboard doors are closed and traffic areas cleared before the light is extinguished. Statistics show that more campers are lost through carelessly placed ice coolers and clotheslines than through crocodile bites.

How to live among our furry friends.

1. Forget Disney. Remember, not all bears have their own television series. Some of them are unemployed wild animals.

2. Never argue with a bear over your picnic basket, even though deep in your heart you know the green onions will repeat on him.

3. Any woman in the laundry room who tries to assure you snakes are as afraid of you as you are of them should be watched.

How to know when you are there.

1. When you are reading the road map and your husband accuses you of moving Lake Michigan over two states.

2. When the kids start playing touch football in the back seat with a wet diaper and the baby is in it.

3. When not only starvation sets in, but your stomach begins to bloat and your vision becomes blurred.

4. When Daddy screams, "Stop kicking my seat!" and the kids are all asleep.

5. When you find a haven the size of a football field that you don't have to back a trailer into (even if it is a football field).

What to do when togetherness becomes an obscene word.

No one, not even a man and a woman, can endure two weeks of complete togetherness—especially when they are married. Thus, being confined with two or three children in an area no larger than a sandbox often has the appeal of being locked in a bus-station rest-room over the weekend. Planning your activities will help avoid this.

1. Keep busy. Rotate the tires on the car. This gets you out in the fresh air and at the same time gives you a feeling of accomplishment.

2. Play games like "Look for Daddy" or "Bury the Motorcycle" (the one that runs up and down through the campgrounds all night).

3. Have a roster of chores. One child could be in charge of water for the radiator. Another could be in charge of killing that last mosquito in the tent at night.

4. Have family dialogues around the campfire. Suggested topics: Who was the idiot who had to bring the ping-pong table and "Harvey, where are you getting the drinking water and what did you hope to find when you put a slideful of it under your new microscope?"

5. Make new friends (assuming your marriage is stable).

If it happens to be Be Kind to Campers Month (July 19–26), observe it by taking a camper to the city for a day.

Maybe other mothers make it to the water skis, but the closest I ever get to water is a laundromat. I have spent entire vacations watching my enzymes and bleach race their way to the dirt and grime in our underwear.

Commercials lie. They always make laundromats seem like fun places where you go around smelling each other's wash, comparing whiteness, looking for hidden cameras, and breaking out in acne at the thought of stubborn stains.

It's not like that at all. There are thirty-eight washes to every washer, sixty-three dryees to each of the three dryers (one of them is out of order) five Coke machines (all of them in order), no chairs, and a small snack table to fold your clothes on.

The "washees" are bustling, no-nonsense people. They stuff the washers, deposit the soap and coins, look at their watches, and estimate they'll be out of there in an hour.

The "dryees" are a bit more affable. They know with three dryers (one of them out of order), they must live as a community for an indeterminate amount of time, striking up acquaintances, laughing, talking, eating, and sometimes intermarrying.

I was lucky. I got in line for a dryer once behind a bearded boy who couldn't have owned more than two pairs of shorts, a T-shirt with the peace sign, and a fringed vest. I figured him for twenty minutes of drying time.

"Why do you suppose the dryers are heating up?" he asked.

"It's all that nerve gas they're dumping in the ocean," I said tiredly.

"Hey, man, I think you're right," he mused. "You come here often?"

"Only when I can slip away," I said.

We talked for another hour or so. Finally, it was his turn. "Hey, Mildred," he shouted across the laundromat. Mildred had four baskets of wet laundry, three children, and five rain-soaked sleeping bags. Her hair was in rollers the size of fruit juice cans. "Wait a minute," she said. "I want to dry my hair first." She started the dryer and stuck her head inside the door.

Later that night I decided to compromise with my husband and go to New York for a vacation.

"That's impossible," said my husband. "Who will sit with the children?"

"My mother," I stated firmly.

"You know how your mother feels about baby-sitting," he said. "After our first child was born, she had her phone and her address unlisted."

That's not exactly true. Mother loves her grandchildren. As she puts it, "I also love Smokey the Bear and Harry Reasoner, but I wouldn't want to sit with them on a regular basis."

She once told me she considered grandchildren a special bonus for having outlived her own children. "When you're a sitting sit-in," she declared, "you lose your role as a grandparent. Of course," she said, "if you get desperate you can call me at this number at a candy store. They know where to reach me."

I called the number. "Mom, I haven't had a vacation away from the kids since my honeymoon."

"What kind of a crack is that?" she asked.

"I told you I was desperate. Do you suppose you could sit with the kids for a few days?"

"They hurt me the last time," she sulked.

"That's my fault," I replied. "I should have told you that when you stand the baby up on your lap, he pushes his head against your chin and severs your tongue in half. Besides, the kids are older now. It'll be easier."

"Than what?" she asked cautiously.

"The problems of teen-agers are overdramatized," I told Mother. "Actually there is nothing to sitting with them. First, I have hidden the distributor from the car in the flour canister. This will give you a warm, secure feeling when the announcer on TV asks, 'It's ten o'clock. Do you know where your children are?' They'll be tearing the house apart looking for the distributor.

"Second, don't worry about meals. They'll eat anything as long as it is in a carry-out bag.

"Third, keep a supply of dimes. You'll need them when you have to make a phone call at the gas station on the corner. Fourth, if you want them to wear something clean, put it in the dirty-clothes hamper. It's sneaky, but it's the only way you can get them to rotate their clothes.

"Fifth, you'll get used to the records, especially if you spend your evenings crouched in the utility closet next to the hot-water heater.

"Sixth, don't ever say you understand them. It breaks down the hostile relationship between you that it takes to understand one another. Now you know all there is to know about the children, I am off to the city."

"Hold it!" shouted Mother. "In case I need you where can I get in touch with you?"

"Here's the number of a candy store," I said. "I'll check in from time to time."

For years, I have tried to figure out the logic of parents who travel on separate airplanes. This is some decision. Do I want to be on the plane that doesn't make it? Or do I want to be left to raise three children alone on an educator's pension?

This is like asking a drowning man if he wants the leaky tire tube or the boat with the hole in it. Either way, you lose.

Frankly, I think it is a theory advanced by airlines to keep women from finding out what Joan Rivers has known for years: The Bunny Club in the sky is a man's world.

I sensed it when my husband and I boarded and I asked the hostess to hang up my white coat that was made out of a perma-wrinkled fabric. She folded it carefully and (excuse the expression) heaved it onto the rack above my head. When my husband boarded she snatched his attaché case out of his hand and started to hang it neatly on a hanger.

"Really," he giggled, "that's not necessary. I can put it under my seat."

"Let me do it, sir," she insisted.

She leaned over and I instinctively threw my shopping bag over her sit-upon. Throughout the trip she was as obvious as a mal bag in the seat pocket.

"Gum? Drink? Pillow? Ice? Dinner? Oxygen? More coffee? Stereo? Magazine?"

"If you play your cards right," I told my husband, "she'll give you a pair of wings and let you drive the airplane."

"She's just being nice," he countered. "She's that way to everyone."

"Oh yeah? Then why did she tell me my seat was a folding chair on the wings?"

We were about twenty-five minutes in the air when we heard the Spanish voices. At first they were faint, but as more people became aware of it, conversation ceased and the voices became more distinct.

Our hostess had just emerged from another costume change when she heard it too. She walked slowly up and down the aisle and stopped at ours. My husband caught her eye and eased the attaché case out from under his seat. He opened it carefully. Through juggling, the switch had been thrown on his tape recorder which contained his Home-taught Spanish records.

"You are the bravest man," said the hostess, grabbing his arm. (What was so brave about apprehending a recording saying, "You are standing on my burro's foot"?)

The rest of the girls crowded around him as though he had just discovered a cure for cracked heels.

On the return flight, we'll be traveling on separate airplanes. I've thought it over. The two alternatives beat this.

I stood on the corner of Seventh Avenue and Forty-second Street in New York at last with my arms outstretched and said to my husband, "You are looking at a woman who has been liberated!"

"Put your arms down before someone puts a cigarette out in your palm," he said dryly.

"Really," I said, "do you realize this is the first time in years we have been on a vacation without the children? No more dried eggs on the dinner plates. No car pools. No telephone. No eating at 3 in the afternoon because of ball practice. We are free! Stand up straight, dear, and don't slouch or your spine will grow that way. What shall we do first?"

"Let's look for a restaurant," he said.

"Good idea. Take Mother's hand before we cross the street. You never know when some crazy man will try to crash a light. Where was I? Oh yes, being free. You know, some women are so child-geared they can't forget they are mothers. This is sad."

"What about this place?"

"It looks all right, but just to be safe order cheese or peanut butter. You can't go wrong with cheese or peanut butter. The men's room is over there. I'll watch your coat. Don't sit on the seat and don't forget to flush."

"Well, I'm back," said my husband. "Did you order?"

"Yes. Did you wash your hands?"

"Really now."

"Here we are. Don't forget your napkin. And don't

talk with food in your mouth. They filled your milk glass too full."

"You don't have to cut my sandwich for me," he said irritably. "I'm quite capable of cutting it myself."

"Habit," I grinned. "Creature of habit. What was I talking about?"

"About being free of the children."

"Speaking of children, did I tell you what your son said when—did you kick me under the table? Now, what does Mama say about keeping your feet on the floor?"

"If God had meant for me to wipe my feet off on people, He'd have made them out of plastic," he said mechanically.

"Right. As I was saying. We have a whole week to be free of kids. Let's go out and do some shopping for them. I saw this four-foot African drum and a Chinese wastebasket with a red dragon on it that would be perfect. I mean if you buy something that fits in your suitcase, they might think we don't love them.

"Isn't it great being liberated?"

I Lost Everything
in the Post-natal Depression

In case you are keeping score, I missed being named Mother of the Year by three votes (all cast by my own children), I was not named to the Olympic Dusting Team, and I was laughed out of the Pillsbury Bake-off. (My husband ate my Tomato Surprise and said, "Why don't you flake off?" and I thought he said "bake off.")

However, at the 1972 meeting of the doctor people in Passaic, New Jersey, I was named as the woman who had the longest post-natal depression period in the history of obstetrics.

After fourteen years, I was still uptight about toilet training, upset because the stretch marks wouldn't tan, and depressed because I was still in maternity clothes.

My favorite story on motherhood came to me through the mail. It involved a mother who had it all together. She was a model of virtue, a paragon of womanhood. She had six children, whom she counseled with great wisdom

and patience. She was never too busy to listen and to talk with in a cool, calm way that was to be envied. She managed her house with quiet efficiency, her personal life with equal stoicism, and she never appeared to be frazzled or overwrought. She thrived on crisis and trauma, smiled in the face of disaster, and through it all remained peaceful and ever-smiling.

One day she was asked how she did it. She was silent for a moment, then she said, "Every evening after the children are in bed, their clothes are laid out for the next morning, their lunches are readied and the lights are out, I fall to my knees beside their beds and say a prayer to God. I say, 'Thank you God for not letting me kill one of them today.'"

Motherhood . . . thy name is frustration.

X-RATED HAIR

Five years ago if someone had told me I would be lending a hair dryer to my son I would have laughed until I got a stitch in my side.

His hair always looked like an unmade bed. The wind parted it. Five fingers combed it. And when birds began to make a nest, we had it cut.

Then one day, all of that changed. The nation went unihair and my son went with it.

It would be nice to report that by this time parents have become acclimated to long hair on their sons. They haven't. Everywhere I go, the first question is, "How long is your son's hair?" I regard the length of his hair as a graph to my parental control over him. In June 1971, I used the heavy-handed parental approach. I told him I did not go through eighteen hours of labor to give birth to a pre-historic Cro-Magnon. He compromised by having the barber wave the scissors over his sideburns.

In September 1971, I used the humiliation route by telling him he looked like Prince Valiant with a two-dollar permanent wave. He was flattered and borrowed my setting lotion.

January 1972 was the year of the direct approach. I set him down and asked him point blank what he was trying to achieve. He said his long hair stood for his individuality. I asked him to get his individuality trimmed as it was falling into his chili. He declined but said he would keep it out of his eyes, which produced an affliction whereby he would snap his neck and for a brief moment you had a clear view of an eyeball.

In March 1972, I decided to compromise. If he would get a haircut, I would let him in the house, reinstate him in the will, and let him put a yellow bug light in his reading lamp. He refused.

This month, I conceded defeat. I told myself that I had seen boys with longer hair (or were they girls?). I told myself that there were worse things than having a son with long hair—like having a tooth grow through your ear, or an eighteen-year-old who wasn't toilet-trained. I told myself I would have to get with it as this is a new generation and they must set their own style. After all, didn't I wear Mickey Mouse hair ribbons? I was in the middle of telling myself that it was a fad and that in a few years he would be as bald as a Marine sergeant, when he went by the door and snapped his neck so that I could see he was conscious.

"Hey, Mom," he said, "we're out of hair spray."

I bit my lip. I'd give it one more try. If chaining him to the bed and playing Wayne King waltzes in his ear doesn't work . . . then I'll adjust.

MOVIE ROULETTE

Something has got to be done about the ratings of movies. No one understands who goes, who waits in the car, who is admitted over sixteen, under seventy-five, or who must be accompanied by Rex Reed.

The way a GP movie rating was first explained to me, it stood for "General viewing with parental consent."

After the first GP movie I saw, I figured it meant Bambi kept his clothes on but he cussed a lot.

Now, after seeing several GP movies with the children, I have come to the conclusion GP means "Go, but Push the Popcorn."

Let me explain. *The Hawaiians* was a GP movie with

Charlton Heston. I trusted Charlton. After all, hadn't he read the Bible on the "Ed Sullivan Show"?

When a woman faced attack on the ship coming over, I shoved our youngest into the aisle and said, "Get some popcorn." When Charlton crawled into bed with Geraldine Chaplin, I turned him around toward the exit and said, "Get more popcorn." As the hero stripped and climbed into a public bath with six or seven nudie natives, I yelled out to the lobby, "More popcorn and wait for fresh butter."

During the showing of *Patton* (which was also a GP), I sent the kid out for popcorn eighty-two times, plus I had him check the pay phones for possible dimes, make sure our car lights weren't on, and check the men's room for his father's Ruptured Duck discharge button from World War II.

My kids say they do more walking during a GP movie than the ushers and besides all the other kids have seen it and said there is nothing wrong with it.

I was reared in a house where my dad canceled *Liberty* magazine because they carried ads for trusses. I was reared in an era where *Gone With the Wind* made headlines because Rhett Butler's parting words were, "I don't give a damn." I was reared in puritanical times when you walked across the street to avoid passing in front of a burlesque house. (Now, they're closing burlesque houses because they can't compete with GP movies.)

I should love to blame somebody . . . anybody . . . for not building censorship into movies. It would be easier. But maybe movie makers are trying to tell us something. Maybe they are putting the responsibility of saying "yes" or "no" back to the parents where it belongs and has always belonged.

I can't tell you how "Donna Reedish" I felt the other night as Mother and I checked out a GP movie the kids wanted to see. The screen was dark and quiet. A couple giggled. I saw them kiss softly.

Mother leaned over and whispered, "Go out for popcorn, Erma." I stomped up the aisle, grumbling, "All the other mothers have seen it and said there was nothing wrong with it!"

THE IMPOSSIBLE DREAM

I never understood why babies were created with all the component parts necessary for a rich, full life . . . with the unfinished plumbing left to amateurs.

If it was a matter of money, there isn't a mother in this world who wouldn't have chipped in a few extra bucks to have the kid completely assembled, trained, and ready to take on long trips.

As it is, mothers stumble along trying to toilet-train their babies by clumsily running water to create an atmosphere and holding sea shells to their ear to suggest rushing water. I used to turn on every faucet in the house and showed slides of Lake Erie while the kid sat there unrolling johnny paper.

I even used to threaten them. I had one kid whom I vowed I would send to the Army with diapers. I threatened him with other things too: a bed with a hole in it, a bicycle with portable plumbing, and an alarm system that rang when wet and lit up a sign on his back that read, LOOK FOR THE RAINBOW.

The whole affair was pretty ridiculous. But then aren't we all when the most important thing in our lives is succeeding vicariously through our children?

Now I note that a new "training kit" has come on the market guaranteed to cut toilet training time up to 90 per cent. (With some kids that adds up roughly to two weeks before football practice.)

It's a little throne with a built-in music box. When the baby has performed . . . and not until . . . the music box rewards him with a little tune.

I first saw it in the bathroom of my next-door neighbor, Gloria.

"Hey, that's terrific," I said. "What does it play?"

" 'The Impossible Dream,' " she said dryly.

"Then, you're having some success with it?" I asked hopefully.

"Not really," she said. "Todd isn't too swift. The first time I put him on, he sat there frozen and scared like he had just been asked to fly the thing to Cuba. So I explained to him, 'Todd, if you do your thing you will hear music.' "

"Did he understand that?"

"Not a word. He sat there a couple of hours and finally

I took him off, went to the kitchen, got a glass of water and poured it into the bowl. The music came out and Todd clapped his hands and danced around like he was seeing the circus for the first time. Then I put him on it again and he sat there for another couple of hours."

"Then what did you do?"

"I took him off and got another glass of water and demonstrated for him again."

"And he finally got the point and now is on his way to being trained, right?"

"Wrong. Every couple of hours or so, he gets a glass of milk and pours it over the potty and dances to 'The Impossible Dream.' "

"Do you think he'll ever be trained?"

"I don't know," she said, sadly shaking her head. "I only know how disappointed he's going to be when he throws a pitcher of water over an Army latrine and there is nothing to dance to."

OBJECTION SUSTAINED

You know the trouble with some women? They have no imagination. A neighbor was telling me the other day that her little boy, Jody, wanted to bring a bull snake home from his vacation.

"What did you tell him?" I asked.

"I couldn't think of a reason why he couldn't," she said, helplessly shrugging her shoulders.

"Are you kidding?" I shrieked. "A few years ago, my son captured a small, slimy specimen in a Coke bottle and I could think of ten reasons for leaving him behind (the snake, not the boy).

"1. Snakes do not know their own minds. They may

jump up and down and think they want to leave their mommies and daddies for a fun trip, but after two days away from home, it's split-up time. (Or spit-up time if they stay)

"2. You would get bored with one another. After all, what can a snake do? Can he chase a ball after you throw it? Can he walk to the shopping center with you on a leash? Can he walk into a crowded room and keep it that way?

"3. Snakes are a minority group. Face it. Do you want him to feel the pains of discrimination? Wouldn't it break your heart to have his admission refused at Bible School? Or leave him outside in a Mason jar while you are inside with friends?

"4. Snakes are difficult to paper-train.

"5. Snakes adhere to a diet of living things. What happens when he runs out of mice and begins to eye our meter reader?

"6. How would you know if he got a headache?

"7. How would you explain it to him if someone accidentally clobbered him with a rake?

"8. You would be forcing on him a monk's existence. How do you know he doesn't want to date and eventually have a family?"

"Did he buy it?" asked my neighbor, bright-eyed. "I mean did he realize that there were inherent differences between a boy and a snake?"

"Not until I hit him with reasons nine and ten."

"Which were?"

"9. If you put that snake in the car with your mother, she will have a heart attack and drop dead.

"10. Ask yourself, do you want to be a motherless boy roaming through life with a sex-starved, militant, maladjusted snake in a Coke bottle?"

"He chose you instead of the snake, right?"

"No, but he's thinking about it."

"GUESS WHO'S STUCK WITH DISHES?"

Fiddler on the Roof holds the all-time performance record for live theater. On Broadway, this is true.

In our home, the record is held by a little drama that unfolds every evening, called, "Guess Who's Stuck with Dishes After Dinner?"

During the past eleven years, the original cast has staged 4,015 performances, plus a matinee on Saturdays and Sundays. The curtain opens to reveal a family sitting around after the evening meal. The oldest child speaks.

"It's your turn," she says mechanically to her brother.

"No way," he says, turning to his brother. "I did them last night."

Little brother turns to the diner on his right and says, "I did them night before last."

"What did we have to eat that night?" challenges his sister, her eyes narrowing.

"We had chicken. I remember because I broke the disposer."

The daughter moves to stage left and shouts, "Then that proves it. We had casserole the night before which I left to soak so that makes tonight *your* night." (She whirls around and points a finger at larger brother.)

"No way," he says. "If you remember I traded you last Tuesday night because you had to decorate the gym."

"And what about that time five years ago when I filled in for you when you broke your arm and spent the night in the hospital?"

"I paid you back for that. Besides, I don't put large mixing bowls in the refrigerator with one prune pit in it to keep from washing, like some people I know."

"And I don't leave my garbage in the sink like other people I know."

Little brother at this point is making a quiet exit stage right when he is discovered.

"*Hold it!* It's your turn. I can tell by looking at you. You are laughing on the inside."

"I am not laughing. I think we should start fresh with the oldest and then keep track."

"You say that because you are the youngest."

"Big deal. I didn't get a watch until I was twelve." (No one has understood that line in eleven years.)

The audience, comprised of two adults, pushes away from the table and walks out of the theater.

"When did we have spaghetti last?" asked my husband.

"About three weeks ago," I said. "Why?"

"I found some on my plate."

"That's what happens when you try to make dishwashers out of sensitive performers."

E IS FOR EAT

The average life span of a refrigerator light is thirty-seven years, four months, and eighteen hours.

We have replaced three bulbs within the last two years. This is due to the fact that every fifteen minutes, the two giant doors swing open (one for the freezer and one for the refrigerator) and my son stands there motionless staring at the contents as though he is awaiting the second coming.

Seeing him look from one side of the box to the other, it always seems as though he should be saying something like, "I suppose you are all wondering why I have gathered you here," but there is nothing. Only cold, silent appraisal.

The other night, as I threw an afghan over my feet to

break the chill from the open refrigerator, I yelled out to him, "Why don't you let those poor leftovers deteriorate in peace?"

"I'm looking for something," he said.

"And you're gonna get it," I threatened. "Now shut that door."

"There's never anything to eat in this house."

"Then how come we are the only six-garbage-can family on our block? Besides, you cannot possibly be hungry. You just got up from the table."

"That was an hour ago."

"Shut the door."

"Can I have an ice cube?"

"I suppose so," I said tiredly. Minutes later, I heard the blender going and went out to investigate. The counter top was spread like a Roman orgy feast with French bread, olives, lunch meat, cheese, dips, and a malt frothing in the blender. "I thought you only wanted an ice cube," I said.

"You can't eat an ice cube by itself," he said, sinking his teeth into a sandwich.

The other night after I had stocked the refrigerator to capacity just three hours before, I too succumbed to the lure of the refrigerator and thought I would open both doors and view the array of food.

To my dismay, I plucked two empty milk cartons from the top shelf, an empty olive jar, a butter carton with no butter in it, a long slice of cheese that was beginning to curl, a cake plate with only a layer of crumbs, the bone of a chicken leg, and a quart-size soft-drink bottle with a cap on it and a quarter-inch of soda in it.

My husband came up behind me. "You too? What's the big attraction?"

I was numb. "I can't believe he ate the whole thing."

FIELD TRIPS

My son entered kindergarten with a four-word vocabulary: "My mom can drive." Later, he added words like "anytime, anywhere, and distance is no object." But for the first year, he made it on those four.

His teacher, Miss Varicose, was quite concerned about him and asked me to come to school to discuss the problem.

"I'm quite puzzled over . . . by the way he never told us his name."

"It's Charlie," I said.

"Charlie seems to be on the outside of our little circle. He does not seek out friends. He never volunteers to answer questions, and at times his behavior is bewildering. For example, the other day I said to the class, 'I want you to line up against the wall, the boys in one line, the girls in another. We are going. . . .' At that moment, Charlie jumped up on the desk, waved his arms excitedly and shouted, 'My mom can drive.'

" 'That won't be necessary,' I told him. 'We are only going to the lavatory.' I don't understand Charlie."

"Of course you don't," I said. "You have to know that Charlie was born on the tail end of our other children, all needing to be driven hither and yon. He was born in a car between helping deliver a Sunday-morning paper route and taking his sister to a Girl Scout cookie rally. He cut his teeth on a stick shift. He learned his numbers by reading the mileage gauge. The only primary colors he knows are red, green, and amber. His alphabet is limited to P, R, N, and D. That kid has spent so much time in a car that when we passed a house the other day, he wanted to know who stole its hubcaps."

"Then being raised in a car has had an effect on Charlie?"

"You didn't notice he holds his pants up with a seat belt?"

"No, I didn't."

"You are not the only one confused, Miss Varicose. Not only for having trouble understanding him, but for the mother image I have created. Most children think of their mothers as hot apple pie and the American flag. Charlie sees me as four wheels and a tank of Platformate. He thinks driving a car is the only thing I can do."

"How did it all begin?" asked his teacher.

"Well, it all began with my first child," I explained. "She came home from school one day bearing a mimeographed sheet of paper. It read:

MOTHERS MOTHERS MOTHERS
WE NEED YOU

The first grade of Bradford Primary will participate in a field trip on Saturday at the Stillwell Owl Sanctuary. We are in need of mothers who can drive. This will be an enriching experience for you.

PLEASE PLEASE PLEASE

"Actually, it wasn't an enriching experience at all. Two of my little passengers entwined themselves around a soft-drink machine and refused to go on the nature walk. One child in the car confided he had chicken pox but his mother covered it up with make-up so he wouldn't miss the field trip. And a flock of owls mistook my car for a relief station and created a credibility gap at the car wash.

"By the time my second child entered school the word

was out. 'My mom can drive,' became their battle cry. It brought them prestige, importance, attention. It brought me girdle creases that can only be removed by surgery. I had so many 'enriching experiences' that the family was eating plastic food and wearing plastic underwear. I took a group to the book bindery, the state gas chamber, the piano factory, the persimmon festival, the press room of a local newspaper, and an aardvark farm.

"One day after returning from a field trip through a steel mill (which was responsible for the fillings in my teeth melting down), my child brought me a mimeographed sheet. 'Guess what, Mom? Our class is going on a boat trip down the river to visit a polo score card factory. I told my teacher, "My mom can drive." '

" 'Not this time,' I sighed, removing my goggles and safety helmet.

" 'Why?'

" 'Really, dear, I mustn't be greedy. There must be thousands of other mothers out there in utility room land who have an enrichment deficiency.'

"His face fell. 'What can I tell my teacher?'

" 'Tell her I am having labor pains thirty seconds apart. Tell her my Mother won't sign my permission slip. Tell her anything.' "

"Did it work?" asked Charlie's teacher, leaning closer.

"No. I ended up driving eight boys and girls to the old Salt Line Pier where we joined forces with eighty other third-graders. The trip was like a Chinese fire drill. Fifty-eight out of the eighty children ate their box lunches before we got out of the school yard.

"Two little girls became nauseated on the boat and threw up in my handbag before we left the dock.

"A kid named Max had me hang onto his water skis which he brought along 'just in case.' Three sweaters, a pair of glasses, and the kid voted most likely to fall overboard fell overboard.

"Linda dropped her loose tooth down the john and became hysterical when the kids told her the tooth fairy couldn't swim.

"The class bully spread a rumor we were on the *Titanic* and had half the class in lifeboats singing 'Nearer My God To Thee.'

"One child swore he saw a ship nearby flying a black flag with Cyril Ritchard aboard. I spent the entire boat trip in the restroom throwing my body in front of obscene words printed in lipstick on the walls.

"When we landed at the factory site, we discovered we had a mutiny on our hands. Two thirds of the children voted to stay in the souvenir shop and buy alligators dressed as merchant seamen and sweatshirts proclaiming, SAVE WATER. TAKE A BATH WITH SOMEONE.

"The other third were bored and wanted to get back to school early so they could shoot baskets in the gym.

"On the trip home, I asked one youngster what he liked best about the trip. He said, 'The towel machine was neat.'

"So you see, Miss Varicose, 'My mom can drive' are the only four words Charlie has heard since he was born and those four words are driving me out of my tree."

"What do you suggest we do?" she asked.

"I was hoping you could work with Charlie and perhaps teach him a new word."

"Like what?"

"Like 'no.' "

"Isn't that rather drastic?" she asked. "I was hoping you might favor the tapering-off plan. You see, this Wednesday our class is going to the museum to see a film on *Birth of a Peat Bog*. No scenes censored. We need mothers to drive. As soon as Charlie discovered it was an enriching experience, he volunteered you. He has the mimeographed sheet telling you to pack a box lunch, wear flats, and be at the school by ten."

"Miss Varicose, what would you say if I told you I was going to put a seat belt around Charlie's mouth?"

"But . . . his pants would fall down. It would be a traumatic experience."

"Better traumatic than enriched."

40 Anonymous

This country is extremely age-conscious. That is why a new group has been formed called "40 Anonymous" to help people overcome the problem. Here's how it works. Several months before reaching age forty, birth-dayees are invited to a group-therapy program.

There is a ten-minute film where Doris Day wrinkles her nose, moistens her lips, and smiles, "I'm over forty and I still have all my own freckles," just to get the audience in a receptive mood. Then a testimonial is given. The one I heard was from Sylvia X.

"I'm over forty," she said in a faltering voice. (Applause) "A few months ago I was depressed and morose and thought life was not worth living. I got a chill when the furnace blower went on. I refused to eat apples even though I had my own teeth. I nipped at Geritol in the mornings after the kids went to school. I sent sympathy cards to myself and refused to start any long novels. A friend suggested I come to a 40 Anonymous meeting. That night I heard Senator Thurmond speak. He was wonderful.

"I went home and practiced saying 'forty' in front of the mirror. I thought I was cured. Then one night I went to a party. Everyone there was under thirty. It was terrible. No one knew the verse to 'Shine on Harvest Moon.' They had never heard of Lyle Talbot or Maria Montez. When I said Okey Dokey, they laughed.

"I went berserk that night and drew a mustache on an advertisement for 'Mod Squad.' A member of 40 Anonymous found me throwing rocks at a rock festival. 'Get hold of yourself,' he said. 'Just say out loud, "I am forty."'

" 'I am foooooffffffffoooorrrr . . . I can't do it,' I cried.

" '*You can!*' he challenged.

" 'It's no use,' I said, 'this world is for the youth. Everyone around me is younger than I am. My doctor carries his stethoscope in a gym bag. My attorney has to shave only once a week. My son's math teacher is still wearing braces. I rode a plane the other day with training wheels on it. Good Lord, man, don't you understand, I am older than Mickey Mouse!' "

Sylvia's voice broke. "Today I am proud to say I have learned to live with my problem one day at a time." (Applause)

That night I stood in front of my mirror and said, "My name is Erma X and I'm fffff. . . . I don't look it, but I'm ffff . . . some days I look . . . ffffoooo . .. last year I was. . . ." It was no use. I called 40 Anonymous. Sylvia came over and had a drink with me.

Actually, forty or any other age wouldn't be so hard to face were it not for the current trend of restaurants making a fuss over birthdays. This ranges anywhere from a drum roll and house lights to a group of waitresses in headbands and adenoids charging at you with a cupcake and a sparkler on top.

I have warned my family if they ever inflict a public birthday on me, I will impale myself on a flaming skewer. After age twelve, birthdays should be as private as hernia surgery. After all, they're as personal.

Philosophers and poets may be as cute as they like about middle age but the question remains, *"What* begins at forty?"

Your laugh lines turn to wrinkles, the dimples in your knees and elbows fill in, you need glasses to read billboards, you find yourself listening to every word of the commercials on motel management and when you at last figure your teen-agers are old enough to be told about sex, you've forgotten what it is you weren't supposed to tell them until they were old enough to be told.

There is little comfort in people like Elizabeth Taylor chirping, "I am not going to fight middle age or wrinkles or fat." (If I had Richard Burton sewed up in my hip pocket, I wouldn't fight anything.)

If I sound bitter, it is because I am going through a phase of middle age known as the "Didn't we go to school together syndrome?" (DWGTSTS)

The DWGTSTS begins on the eve of your fortieth birthday and continues until no one wants to claim you as a contemporary. I have never had so many bald, paunchy individuals accost me and invite me to remember the good old days. (And those are the women.)

The other night at a restaurant a Sun City Freshman stopped by our table and said, "Remember me? We were in cooking class together."

I looked up, shocked. When this woman was in cooking class, fire hadn't been invented yet. "It's Edna something or other, isn't it?" she persisted. "And you used to write for the school paper."

"You're thinking of Edna St. Vincent Millay," I said stiffly.

"No," she said, "your hair is a little different color, your teeth look different, you're wearing glasses and carry a little more weight, but I'd know you anywhere."

"What gave me away?" I asked my husband.

"The way your eyes lit up when the orchestra played 'Beer Barrel Polka.'"

It's occasions like that that make you swear off high school reunions. If you're keeping track I have just gone to my last one.

It's not fair to all those balding, aging, dissipated, frumpy, flabby, graying people wandering around trying to be cheerful, when I look so great.

I found myself walking up to classmates, saying, "What happened?"

Take poor Clara what's-her-name. Her memory is shot. She went around all night calling me Ernie. Serves her right for marrying old Charley . . . or was it Harley what's-his-face.

As for poor Iris Pick, I could have wept for her. Had three children, bang, bang, bang. They drive her out of her tree. Lucky my three are spaced better.

The real shocker was our valedictorian, Enis Ertle. She's absolutely out of it. If the President had been there she'd have gone up and asked, "What are you doing these days?" I told her I'd give her my copy of *Peyton Place* when I finished reading it.

And if anyone had told me my best girl friend, Wanda Weight, would be nearly white-haired, I wouldn't have believed it. My wig nearly fell off when I saw her. Everyone was saying my old boy friend, Leroy Katch, looked positively prehistoric. I couldn't find my glasses in the bottom of my handbag to see for myself, but I can't imagine they would lie.

As I told my husband on the way home, "It's incredible to imagine some of our classmates are grandparents."

"I know," he said quietly.

"Do you know what that means?" I asked. "It means some of them had to have their children when they were mere babies of. . . ."

"Twenty-five," he said.

"It's funny about the teachers though," I commented. "Miss Kravitz looked seventy years old when I had her for Social Problems. Tonight she looked only about fifty. You're quiet. Anything wrong?"

"Nevin Noose came up with a mouthful of false teeth. I nearly dropped my partial."

"Couldn't you cry for them?" I said sadly. "Poor devils fighting middle age. We shouldn't have gone, but I wanted to see them all again before they got too old to appreciate me."

People do approach milestones in their own particular way.

On my husband's fortieth birthday, he locked himself in his bedroom with a copy of *Playboy* magazine and made an obscene phone call to Ted Mack.

That's the way fortieth birthdays are.

I knocked on the door and pleaded, "Why don't you come out and show us your presents? I want to see what the kids got you?"

The door opened a crack and he said, "Come in."

"I know they got you a bottle of hair creme," I said, "but what kind? Torrid Torment? Show No Mercy? Shameless Interlude?"

"No," he said, shaking his head vigorously.

"What then? Frankly Intimate? Sextop for Pop?"

"Let me say it is something I can handle," he said, clearing his throat nervously.

"It's not one of those things you're going to have to fight your way on and off buses with, is it? Or karate chop your own mother?"

"I know what I'm doing," he said. As he scooped his boxes, tissue and ribbon up in his arms, the box of hair creme fell to the floor. I picked it up and read the name "Resignation Hair Creme," and in small letters below it claimed, "For the man who has everything but hair. No sexy aroma. No tantalizing softness to run your hands through. No double takes from girls on the beach. Resignation Hair Creme just keeps your head from getting chapped."

"I guess that's all the kids could buy without a prescription," I alibied.

"I guess so," he replied softly.

He moped around for several months after that. Then, along came the football season and George Blanda. For all of you who think football is a winter replacement for the summer reruns, George Blanda is the world's oldest quarterback. He is forty-four years old. At a time of his life when he should be sitting in the stands with a thermos of hot chicken soup, he is sparking the Oakland Raiders to some unbelievable victories.

Well, I can't begin to tell you what George Blanda did for my husband.

When George kicked a forty-eight-yard field goal against Kansas City for a tie, my husband kicked off his lap robe (he was sitting in the living room by the fire) and said, "I think tomorrow I'll jog to the garbage can and back."

When George kicked a fifty-two-yard field goal to win the game with Cleveland 23-20, my husband kicked his Geritol bottle thirty-two feet into the air. When Blanda whipped out a twenty-yard touchdown pass with only seconds to go to beat Denver 24-19, my husband ambled through the living room and announced loudly, "I am donating my Supp-hose to Goodwill."

George Blanda was Lydia Pinkham to my husband. Then the new neighbors moved in next door and we were back to where we started.

"What are they like?" I asked as he came back across the lawn.

"Young," he snarled.

"How young?"

"He can still get his car in the garage."

"What about his wife?"

"She was waxing the garden hose."

"What did you talk about?"

"Don't ask. I made the mistake of telling him I was in the Army. He said his grandfather was in World War II and they studied it a lot in college. I tell you, it was incredible. He had never heard of victory gardens, Senator Joe McCarthy, Glenn Miller, Snooky Lansen, the twist, Ozzie and Harriet, Packards, the Brooklyn Dodgers, or Fred Allen."

"It won't be easy. Do they have any children?"

"No. He said he and his wife decided not to have any in view of the fact they were concerned with overpopulation and what do you call it?"

"Copping out?"

"No . . . ecology."

"Do they play bridge?"

"No. He said it was frivolous in this time of involvement, when everything else needed his attention. I don't want to frighten you, but I think he's going to take sex education out of the home and put it on the ballot where it belongs. And she's a feminist who is going to picket the Avon lady."

"What do they do for kicks?"

"I think they sit around and watch each other's hair grow."

"You're being unkind. We were that young once."

"I was born older than they are," he sulked.

"Why, I remember the first time my grandmother met you," I said. "When you turned your back she said to me, 'He's a funny-looking thing, but when he grows hair, he might look all right.' "

"I had a burr haircut. It was the style," he shouted.

"I know. And we didn't know anything about Tom Mix, Will Rogers, the League of Nations, the cakewalk, Gene Fowler, and the Reo Runabout."

"I suppose you're right," he sighed, "but when people start moving next door to you who have never heard of Fred Allen. . . ."

"There goes the neighborhood," I said sadly.

On my fortieth birthday, my family chipped in and bought me a tennis racket. I don't wish to sound ungrateful, but this is like buying the Pope a Mouseketeer beanie.

"When are you going to use it?" the kids kept clamoring.

"When it snows and I get another racket to put on the other foot," I said.

The truth is, I have never cared for sports that take me away from the table. (Besides, I tire easily and tend to black out when I spend an evening licking Green Stamps.)

But these obstacles were small compared to the prejudice I encountered when I ventured to the tennis courts with my brand-new racket and my old body.

There is no evidence to sustain this, but I have a feeling new tennis rackets secrete an odor that is detected within a fifty-mile radius by experienced tennis players. The moment you appear, men in white shorts hurry toward their cars, women in white tennis dresses sniff the air and mumble something about burning dinner, and even small children playing in their bare feet back off and say, "I think I hear my mother calling."

I found one young man trying to scale the fence and said, "Would you like to play a game?"

"Have you ever played tennis before?" he asked.

"No," I giggled, "What gave me away?"

"Your sweat band. You don't wear it to the armpits."

"But that is where. . . ."

"You wear it around the wrist. Listen, I gotta cut out. Some other time. . . ."

The next night I went down again and this time collared a twelve-year-old girl who tripped and fell as the rest of the players ran from the courts to their cars.

"What am I doing wrong?" I asked.

"First, you don't get a new suit if you hit the ball over the big fence. That's baseball. Next, you don't get an extra point if you hit the drinking fountain. And take the press off your racket when you play."

During the next few weeks, I worked like a demon to shake the new-racket stigma . . . playing with anyone I could trap.

The other day I ambled onto the courts and there was this tired-looking housewife in pedal pushers and a Howard Hughes sweatshirt.

"Have you ever played tennis before?" I asked.

She shook her head. "How can you tell?"

"You don't wear the sweat band around your ankle, dear. I gotta go. I hear the timer on my stove going off. . . ."

Actually, my physical shape isn't the only thing that bothers me about my twilight years.

A scientist in California has figured out that every day after thirty-five, the adult loses 100,000 brain cells which affect thinking and memory.

My kids would argue that the loss is considerably higher than this. Since age thirty-five, I haven't had an original thought, done anything significant and while others were making giant steps for mankind, I was making giant steps with the garbage.

To prove to you this is not an idle observation, I took the trouble to keep a diary for an entire week, during which time I scientifically dropped 700,000 brain cells.

Monday: Twelve-year-old working on an English assignment asked me who the Earl of Sandwich was. When I suggested he was the one who always carried his lunch to the castle, twelve-year-old shook his head and said, "I'll call up one of the guys."

Tuesday: Reached a high level of incompetence by absentmindedly pouring powdered milk in dishwasher dispenser. Daughter suggested a companion to sit with me all day until Daddy could relieve her in the evening.

Wednesday: Heard a suspicious rattle in the car.

Drove it into the service station where they discovered an aerosol can of de-icer rolling around near my spare tire. I am permitted to drive now only if accompanied by a teen-ager.

Thursday: Was called upon to determine the sex of our hamster, which I did without hesitation, claiming no mating was possible. Male hamster is now in maternity tops.

Friday: Missed taking my discarded chicken innards from the freezer and putting them in garbage, thus bringing the total of chicken innards in my freezer to 320 pounds.

Saturday: Mental deterioration noted as someone mentioned having a paternity suit and I said I hoped they didn't catch on because I don't have the legs to wear them.

Sunday: Family found me laughing hysterically over Tom Jones singing, "I Who Have Nothing." Family saw no humor in it and concluded I should be sent to a church camp.

The scientist from California is on to something. He has already figured out the brain drain is caused by aging, impaired circulation, and other causes. He has not figured out why thirty-five is the magic year for deterioration.

Even in the prime of my senility, I figured that one out.

At thirty-five most parents launch their first teen-ager. After that, professor, it's Bananasville all the way.

As far as my memory is concerned, as I was telling my husband, what's-his-name, "I've got to do something about my memory."

"Why?" he asked.

"Why what?"

"Why do you have to do something about your memory?"

"Oh, I don't know. Just little things have been getting

by me lately. Like letting your insurance policy lapse
. . . and forgetting Christmas the way I did and the
humiliating thing that happened to me at the airport last
week."

"What humiliating thing?" he asked, putting down his
paper.

"Well, I was saying good-by to your sister when I saw
this man smiling at me and he looked so familiar and I
was sure I knew him, but I just couldn't put a name to
him. So, just to be safe I ran over and grabbed his hand,
pumped it and said, 'Gosh, it's good to have you home
again. We've all missed you. As soon as you're settled,
call and we'll get together for dinner.' "

"What's the matter with that?"

"In the car coming home I remembered who he is. It
is Mr. Whitlock, the man who cleans our septic tank
every year."

"It could happen to anyone," he said sympathetically.

"I suppose so. But ever since I took a memory quiz
that appeared in the newspaper last week I've been real
concerned."

"What quiz?"

"It's good to know someone else has a rotten memory.
Don't you remember? It's the article I clipped out just
before you got the paper. Here it is:

"1. When you cannot remember where you parked
your car in town do you (a) have total recall of your
make of car, serial number, and license plates, or (b)
take a bus home and pretend it doesn't matter?

"2. At class reunions, do you (a) use the Association
Method to remember names (i.e., he is hairy and
paunchy; ergo, his name is Harry Paunchy), or (b) do
you squint at name tags upside down and say, 'Nayr
Mot, long time, no see'?

"3. Do you (a) have specific places for your sewing
basket, office equipment, cleaning supplies, and cooking

utensils, or (b) are you content to put in hems with Band-Aids and take down phone messages using a cuticle stick on wax paper?

"4. Do you (a) keeps tabs on your grocery shopping cart by remembering its contents, or (b) do you have to 'mark it' by forcing your twelve-year-old to sit in the basket in a fetal position?

"5. Do you (a) always remember the ages, sex, names, and grades of your children, or (b) do you have to stop and count backward or forward the year the cat came to live with you?

"6. Do you (a) always repeat the name of the person you are introduced to, or (b) repeatedly look perplexed and say 'Abigail *Who?*'

"7. Do you (a) always make a note in your checkbook of the amount of the check and to whom it was made out at the time you are writing the check, or (b) do you tell yourself that you'll do it later when you're not in such a hurry?

"You know what I think the trouble is?" I asked, folding the paper. "I share my house with four disorganized people. It isn't easy trying to keep everything in a place with everyone going in separate directions. For example, the other day I opened the tea canister and some clown had put tea in it."

"That's wrong?" asked my husband.

"That's wrong!" I shouted. "So where's my rice now? And speaking of boots, do you know how long it took me to find the kids' boots the other morning?"

"I can't imagine."

"Three hours. And just because some ding dong took them out of the soft drink cooler in the garage and didn't put them back. I suppose I could be like Doris you-know-who."

"You mean my sister?"

"Yes. She's so organized she makes me sick. I was in

her house the other day and she had a pad and pencil right next to the phone. Can you imagine that? And when she wants a needle she doesn't have to have kids run through the carpets in their bare feet. She keeps them in a package with her thread. (The needles, not the kids.) And here's the zinger. She keeps her car keys on a little hook in the utility room so she always knows where they are. Oh well, what can you expect from a woman who numbers her checks consecutively?"

"Don't you keep your car keys in the same spot?" he asked.

"Are you kidding? If it weren't for looking for my car keys I'd never know where anything is. Take the other day. I was looking for the keys in the trunk of the car where I always leave them and found my new sweeper bags.

"When I went to put the sweeper bags on the broom-closet shelf, I found my rain hat which I haven't seen in two years. And when I went to put the hat in the coat closet I discovered my checkbook, which had been missing.

"While returning the checkbook to the stove drawer where it belongs, guess what? There were the scissors I had been searching for during the last week. I returned the scissors to the bookcase where I hide them from the kids, and found my dental appointment, which I had been using for a bookmark. I always keep my dental appointment in my jewelry box, so when I dropped it in there, lo and behold, there was the freezer key."

"And where are the car keys?" asked my husband.

"Well, if you can't find yours either," I sighed, "maybe I'm not as bad off as I thought."

Minutes later the phone rang. As I replaced the receiver I said, "Hey, guess who's coming to dinner Saturday? Wilma and Leroy Whitlock. You wanta give me hint? Who are *they*?"

Who Packed the Garbage?

We had a couple of good years in our house, then it happened. The rooms shrank, the cupboards disappeared, and the schools and the shopping centers moved. The lawn spread, the closets diminished, and no one could find the garage that the buyer swore went with the house. "Maybe we could start looking for a larger house," I suggested.

"Indeed not," said my husband. "I am sick and tired of moving every time the ashtrays fill up. We stay!"

He would need a little convincing.

"Why am I sleeping with the storm windows?" he asked one morning.

"You devil, you noticed," I said.

"I noticed. Why am I sleeping with the storm windows?"

"It's a mistake," I said. "The boys are supposed to sleep with the storm windows. You're supposed to sleep with the bicycles. There's no storage space in this house."

"You're as subtle as bad breath," he said. "We stay."

"I love these advanced schools out here," I continued. "Did I tell you the primary grades are putting on *The Last Picture Show* for a Christmas pageant?"

"We stay," he persisted.

"I hope you're not in your safe office worrying around about us all day in a house with a front door that won't lock, a clogged-up flue, an overloaded kitchen circuit, and Smokey the Bear posting signs all over the attic.

"The front spigot is broken, the lawn is ridden with crab grass, two dining room windows are stuffed with paper towels, the front door snaps behind you like a trap, the bathroom tile is rusting, and I took the Sears catalogue out of the bathroom. When the wind whistles down the vent. . . ."

"Maybe we'd better start looking around. . . ."

"I've already written the ad," I smiled. " 'Charming three-bedroom home in the suburbs you have to see to believe. Spacious rooms, storage, fireplace, two baths, many extras. Convenient to progressive schools and shopping center. Will sacrifice to family who promises to love it.' What are you doing?"

"I'm making a list of the things that have to be done. I had no idea the house was that bad. Where's your pride, woman? Do you want people to think we live this way?"

Later that night we read the ad. "I'll miss your home-made screens. Remember the night we almost named a mosquito in our divorce suit?"

"That was nothing compared to the day we hung wallpaper in the hallway. And your daffodil bulbs. Remember? You planted them upside down and they haven't surfaced yet."

"I love this kitchen. The trees are just beginning to look finished. We brought three babies to this happy house."

"I hope no one buys it," he said.

"Me too," I sobbed.

Our sentiment gave way to practicality a few days later. As you know there are two methods of selling one's house. You can try to sell it yourself or contract an agent to do it for you.

Real estate agents tell you if you attempt to do it yourself you will be badgered by phone calls, hounded by curiosity seekers, and driven crazy by Sunday lookers. They are right.

The first day our ad appeared we were badgered by eight agents on the phone, hounded by five agents who were curiosity seekers, and driven crazy by real estate agents who were Sunday lookers.

We were also discouraged by our homemade tours. Lord knows we tried. I would gather a couple of live ones in the hallway (my husband threatened to start biting his nails again if I involved him in my little off-Broadway production) and give them a brief history of the house.

I cautioned them about staying with the guide and reminded them that the closets would be opened only upon a written request submitted twenty-four hours in advance of the tour.

Some groups were quite ugly. When I gestured toward the lavatory and announced, "This is the bathroom," one fat man with a cigar snarled, "You're kidding! I thought it was a mess kitchen with a crazy soup pot!"

Some women, I discovered, made a profession of touring houses for sale. It was something to do on grocery day, like trying on hats in the dime store or looking at trusses in the medical-supply house.

We finally put the house in the hands of our friendly real estate agents. From that moment the family was on red alert.

When the agent called to say she was bringing a prospective customer through, one child would empty

ashtrays, gather all the dishes off the table, and dump them in the oven. (Later we found people look in ovens, so we stored them in the back seat of the car.) One would smooth the empty beds, put out fresh towels, and empty waste cans.

Another would cover the bird, tie up the dog, and douse the hamster cage with a strong deodorant. I would pull down the garage door, unscrew the bulb in the utility room, prop a few crummy plastic flowers in the bathroom, and as my last act on the way out . . . flush.

Satisfied that the house looked as if it had never been lived in, we scurried to the neighbor's spirea bushes where we stayed until the entourage left.

This went on for weeks. The strain was beginning to

show on all of us. Then one night it happened. We showed the house with the kids in it . . . sitting on the sofa . . . with all the lights on. This was the night the house sold.

I felt a quiet giddiness and relief, like when you think you're pregnant and it turns out to be Asian flu. I was smiling out loud when my husband walked in.

"You know the garage that's been missing since we bought the house? I just found it under some junk. As they say in the ads, 'You have to see it to believe it.' "

If selling the house was traumatic, moving made me a prime candidate for the Mental Health poster girl of the month.

Once when I was a kid I remember the circus came to town. Within minutes of the finale, the big tent was hauled down and loaded on a train. Aboard were 15 trained elephants, 5 wild lions, 2 domestic bears, 12 dancing ponies and a singing prairie dog all caged neatly in a row, and 250 performers and workers who waved good-by from the train as they pulled out of town.

It took me *three weeks* to make contact with my friendly moving representative.

He gave me a manual, *Everything You've Always Wanted to Know About Moving but Were Too Cheap to Ask,* that said there was nothing to it. In the foreword it said, "One out of every five families in the United States moves every year. (See page 117 for illustration.)"

I turned quickly to page 117, where a picture brought tears to my eyes. Mother was playing checkers on a moving box with her pre-schoolers. Dad, with a pipe in his mouth, was bouncing a beach ball to his son, while in the background six movers were earning hernias.

The manual continued, "Remember the three key concepts of a fun move: Planning, Organization and Ruthlessness with Your Discards."

"If you want to stand around and bounce a beach ball to your son on moving day," I announced to my husband, "you are going to have to plan."

"What does that mean?" he asked.

"That means I have already packed your golf clubs, electric shaver, books and clothes, with the exception of a pair of slacks, three shirts, and change of shorts."

"But we're not moving for five weeks!"

"That's where organization takes over," I said. "You will note that each box which is packed has a number on it from one to nine. Each number corresponds with a master sheet on which each room in the new house is given a number. Thus, when the mover walks in the front door and says, 'Number Five, lady,' I will look up from my checkers game and say softly, "That's the second bedroom on the right, down the hall.' "

"Where's the master sheet?" he asked.

"I'm not sure," I pondered. "It's either packed in a Number One box with unpaid bills and unopened fourth-class mail or it is stuffed inside an encyclopedia in a banana box that I got from the A&P. It will show up. Don't worry. In the meantime, we must work on being ruthless with our discards."

We had never been ruthless with our discards before. We discovered that when we ran across three boxes in the attic marked, RAIN-SOAKED HALLOWEEN MASKS.

"I say we can do without your attendance certificates from the third grade and your leather desk calendar from 1954," I said, blowing dust from a carton in the attic.

"Very well," he retaliated, "I say we can do without your broom with four straws and a dress form that hasn't fit you since you were ten."

"Okay," I growled, "it's out with your torn billfold with the autographed picture of Gale Storm."

"Then it's *out* with that box of baby things with the milk-stained bibs."

"Now, just a darned minute," I said. "Any mini-brain knows that you do not throw out baby clothes."

"Why not?"

"Because you're asking for it, that's why. I knew a woman who gave away her baby clothes and the next month she became pregnant."

"What's wrong with that?"

"She was fifty-three years old!"

During the next few weeks we were to devote every waking hour to disposing of our disposables. It took us a day and a half to lug all the stuff from the attic to the end of the driveway. It took our kids just twenty minutes to bring it all inside again. (The baby just sat in the middle of the floor in a Mouseketeer beanie clutching a consumptive basketball and looking hostile.)

Aganist my better judgment we even staged a garage sale that made Disneyland look like a mausoleum.

The whole idea was conceived by my girl friend Esther, who said, "You are a natural for a garage sale."

"Why do you say that?" I asked.

"Because you are cheap."

"I don't think you understand," I sniffed, "that spreading one's personal wares out in a garage for public exhibition is not only crass, it smacks of being tacky."

"I made thirty-two bucks off my junk," she said.

"Why didn't you say so?" I asked excitedly. "Get the card table and let's get started."

The garage sale began at 9 A.M. By 7:30 A.M., I had fifteen cars parked on the driveway, eighteen on the lawn, two in a ditch, and a Volkswagen trying to parallel park between two andirons in my living room.

They grabbed and bought anything that wasn't pumping water, cemented in the ground, growing from seed, or spit sparks at them when touched.

They bought cocktail toothpicks that were billed, "Like new" . . . radios guaranteed not to play ever . . .

plastic flowers that had died . . . toothless rakes . . . buckets with leaks . . . books of German military commands . . . and a ukelele that only knew one song, "The World Is Waiting for the Sunrise."

At one point I tried to shove through the crowd with a package in my hand. A woman grabbed it from me and said, "I'll give you thirty-five cents."

"No, really," I stammered, "this isn't . . ."

"Forty cents," she said, grabbing it, "and that is my last offer."

It is the first time anyone ever paid me forty cents for my garbage.

By 4 P.M. I watched tiredly as a woman tried to coax my husband into her trunk.

"Esther," I said, "this is the most incredible sight I have ever seen."

"What's in that package under your arm?" she said.

"It's nothing," I hesitated.

"It's mildewed laundry," she shouted. "How much did you pay for it?"

"Thirty-five cents, but some of it still fits."

With the garage sale behind us, all that remained was the checklist the moving representative had given us.

"You want to read it aloud," I asked my husband, "while I confirm it?"

"I can't," he said. "You packed my glasses away five weeks ago."

"Oh, for crying out loud. I'll read and you check. Did we turn off the milkman? Telephone? Furnace? Utilities? Newspaper? Garbage? Mail?"

"Check."

"Did we defrost the refrigerator? Unplug the washer? Disconnect the Avon lady?"

"Check."

"Did we change our address on magazine subscriptions, insurance policies and credit cards?"

"Check."

"Do we have all of our valuables including jewelry, stocks, checks, cash, and important papers in one place?"

"They're in my shirt pocket," he said dryly.

"Can you drive with the tropical fish on your lap and a potbound philodendron at your feet?"

"I think so."

"Did we ever find the front door key?"

"Did we ever have one?"

"I guess that's it," I said, smiling. "I have the checkerboard and the beach ball. All we have to do is find the car keys and the kids and. . . ."

We both looked at each other at the same time. Then we started ripping cardboard boxes open.

"Could they be packed in a Number Two box with the cocktail olives and used razor blades?"

"Try the Number Five Box marked 'Faded Towels and Shirt Cardboards for Finger-painting. . . .'"

Actually, this wasn't the first time we had ignored the children in the whole operation. When we made plans to move, it never occurred to us to discuss it with our children. We knew our older son would follow the refrigerator into combat if he had to. Our daughter makes her residence behind the wheel of a compact, so it was just a matter of finding a home for her mouthwash. And we had raised our younger son with a two-word philosophy, "Trust us."

Then, a woman at the dry cleaners said, "I cannot believe you did not call a family council and discuss it with your children. Moving a child against his will often makes a psychological imprint that is difficult to heal."

"I don't know about you," I said, as we gathered around the dining room table, "but I feel like Ozzie and Harriet voting on whether or not to have the fruit punch or the Shirley Temple fizzie at the fraternity sock hop."

My husband cleared his throat. "I suppose you wonder why I have gathered you all together. We are moving in a few weeks and wanted to encourage some discussion on it."

My son ate an apple noisily (core and all) and said it was all right with him and left. My daughter asked us to leave the new address in the sun visor of the car and made her exit. Our youngest son said simply, "I'm not going."

"WHATYA MEAN YOU'RE NOT GOING!" we shouted.

"I've thought it over," he said, "and I've got too much going for me here. My friends . . . my school . . . my paper route."

"But where would you live?" we asked.

"I could get an apartment."

"A twelve-year-old in an apartment. You can't even ride your bike across the highway."

"I thought family councils were supposed to be democratic," he said.

"They are," barked his father, "and if you still have

relatives living in town you want to see again, be quiet."

"You and your crummy democratic way," I said, "I told you it wouldn't work."

His father took a deep breath and steadied himself against the table. "As council president, I move to motion that discussion on the matter of moving be closed and any objections must be submitted in writing before the next council meeting which has been indefinitely suspended. The family council is adjourned."

We both sat there. "Wonder what a psychological imprint looks like?" I asked my husband.

"I don't know," he said. "The only thing I can remember from my father is a hand imprint on my hindside that stayed red for a year and a half. It's probably the same thing."

We spent all of our time being apprehensive about traveling across country with three hostile children. We should have given more time to thinking about traveling with a dog.

I've read about people who simply will not travel unless they can take their animals with them.

But then, I've also read about monks who flog themselves with chains for penance, and a native tribe in New Zealand that inflicts pain by wearing spears through their tongues.

I am as crazy about animals as the next one, but face it, following a moving van 3,000 miles with a dog's rump in your face, and his ears whipping your face as they flap in the no-draft is no way to travel. We were not on the road with our dog eight hours before we realized he placed certain restrictions on everyone in the car.

1. He demanded a seat of his own. In the front. Next to the window. With his own safety belt.

2. When another car passed with a dog in it, he declared the car open range and sprang from the front

to the back seat, gouging everyone with his toenails and obstructing everyone's view. (My husband remembers the entire state of Texas as a hairy tail.)

3. There would be none of this crack-the-window-and-leave-the-dog-in-the-car-while-we-eat routine. The first time we tried it his screams were picked up by a Russian satellite. From then on, he ate hamburgers, fries, chicken, pizza, and tacos with the rest of the people.

4. He was quite selective about his rest-rooms, rejecting the barren strips along the roadside, open field, and secluded forests. He preferred the intimacy of a lawn chair at poolside, a potted plant in the motel lobby or the leg of a hotel manager.

"The problem," said my husband one night at the motel, "is the dog has nothing to do."

"He chewed up the last three coloring books I bought him," I said dryly, "and he doesn't sing well."

"Don't be cute," he said. "I feel sorry for him. I think the answer is to stop more often and let him run and be with other dogs."

The next afternoon we pulled up to a roadside park and followed the signs to a section marked, DOG AREA. The grass was so tall we could barely find the picnic table. Delicately, we made our way through where we found ourselves surrounded by dogs.

"This is great," said my husband. "Just what he needs. Now where's the dog?"

We looked around to discover him in the well-manicured lawn section sitting on a bench eating fried chicken with an older couple.

I shook my head. "I know he's a dog. You know he's a dog. Do you want to tell him and break his heart?"

We had three thousand miles to talk about the house we wanted. A friend who is an Air Force wife says there is nothing to reading ads in the newspapers. You just have to speak the language. Once you break the language code salesmen use in selling houses, it's no sweat. For example:

"A Handyman's Dream." If you're married to a contractor, buy it. If not, forget it. Chances are the last major repair on the house was a new chain for the john.

"Spacious Grounds and Green Grass." This means the septic tank is gone. To be sure, check out the house during a drought. If there is an oasis, pass it by.

"Tenants Leaving City—Immediate Occupancy." They don't tell you the former occupants were a motorcycle gang who left skid marks on the living room floor and used the dumbwaiter for beer cans.

"No Children." Show me a landlord who will not accept children and I'll show you a landlord who doesn't permit squeaky rockers, asthmatic coffeepots, heel plates on your loafers, or flushing after 5 P.M.

"You've got to see it to believe it." You do and you won't.

"Priced for quick sale." Watch out for these, especially if the owners wish to be paid in pesos.

"Southern Charmer. Built in 1732." The plumbing was built in 1732. The rest was patched up with defense-cabin leftovers.

"Country Living." Yes, but which one? We once lived in a house so far out of town, we had to get malaria shots.

"Convenient to Stores." It's usually over one.

Another pitfall we had to watch out for was neighborhoods. I guess there are some naïve women who think that when you buy a home you consider only its physical features, its distance from good schools, and its convenience to shopping centers.

Rarely do they interview their prospective neighbors until they have an unpleasant experience. When I was first married, I fell into a "bad neighborhood." I discovered one of my neighbors baked bread. Another was a size three who did not go into maternity clothes until she was 8½ months. (My stomach was larger than hers when I coughed.) And she dusted her mailbox.

Four years ago I hit it lucky. We bought a house between two cemeteries. But then, how often do those opportunities come along?

That's why I think it's a good idea to do a "home study" on a neighborhood before you find yourself in a nest of thin, intelligent, talented, organized mothers, who are also athletic. (If the good Lord had meant for me to play tennis, he would have divided my legs from the hips to the knees.)

Before I buy I always ask them to answer true or false to the following: Ovens with see-through doors should be banned.

Surplus kids should be recycled in the name of ecology.

Christmas tinsel in the rug is a lived-in home.

A small waist makes you tire easily.

A well-balanced meal is boring.

Eliminate clutter. Get rid of your sweeper attachments.

If you have checked true to each of these, I wish you lived in my neighborhood.

We looked at one house and I saw a neighbor out of doors. As we were talking, one of her children came up and asked, "Mom, did you iron my plaid skirt?"

"Of course," smiled the mother patiently, "it's hanging in your closet, dear."

"But are you sure you ironed it?" insisted the child. Her mother nodded. "Okay," said her daughter. "It's just that I'm not used to a cold zipper."

Now there's a neighbor I could love.

It's hard to believe that we bought the new house in three days.

Unless your marriage was made in heaven, I do not

recommend it. We have always adhered to a theory that the union of two people was never meant to withstand the punishment of (1) hanging wallpaper together, (2) pruning shrubbery side by side, (3) working as a team on the checkbook, (4) sharing an electric blanket with a single control, (5) spending three rainy days in a camper, or (6) having children ten and a half months apart.

We have just added to this list (7) buying a house. Being extremely efficient, my husband kept a notebook of the dozen or so houses we viewed and at the end of the day in our hotel room, we would go over the day's crop.

"The one with the woman cleaning the pool was well built," said my husband.

"The house?"

"No, the woman."

"Personally," I said, "I like the house with the meatloaf in the oven. There's something about onions. . . ."

"Was that the one where the owner kept following us around and pointing, 'This is the bathroom'?"

"Yes, and you were rude to keep shouting, '*Right.*' I loved the decorator's house, but it was too small. How old is Junior now?"

"Forget it. He's only twelve and isn't even engaged."

"I liked the one with the basketball hoop," said a voice.

"Who's he?" I asked tiredly.

"Our twelve-year-old," said my husband.

"We've got to start narrowing it down," I sighed.

"Okay, I vote for the house on that deserted dirt road," he grinned.

My eyes flashed. "You won't be happy until I have to organize a garbage car pool, will you? Why don't we get that long ranch house from that adorable woman who had my book on her coffee table?"

"Our furniture wouldn't fit into that house."

"Since when does Early Poverty fit *any* house?" I snarled. "Did the house with the vicious dog do anything for you?"

"I couldn't see much from the car with the windows rolled up," he said. "Besides I'm thinking we had better give up buying and look for a rental."

"That tears it," I snarled. "We look at thirty-one houses in three days, count bathrooms, check out plumbing, interrupt dinners, make pages of notes, and you suggest renting. That's what you can expect, I guess, from a man whose mother wore a navy blue dress to our wedding."

"We'll buy the one with your book on the coffee table."

I threw my arms around him. "Wonderful. You may have to sleep with the storm windows for a while until we can figure out storage, and if it doesn't work out, we can always shop for another house. . . ."

She Has a Cold. Shoot Her.

When women's lib comes out for Equal Colds, I will join it.

I never minded dancing backward . . . or having buttons on the wrong side of my blouse, or having to ask for a key every time I want to go to a service-station restroom. But just once I would like to have my cold given the same respect as a man's cold.

A few weeks ago when my husband had the sniffles, he took his cold to his bed, summoned three medical opinions, insisted I mail the children out of the state, installed a dumbwaiter in his bedroom (me!) and wrote to ABC insisting he would make a great two-part series for "Marcus Welby, M.D."

Two days ago, I awoke to pain. My head was feverish, my lips cracked. My throat was dry. I was nauseated. Every bone in my body begged to be put to rest. "I do not feel well," I said to my husband. "In fact, I don't mean to be dramatic, but think I am dying."

"Does that mean you're not going to get dressed?" he asked impatiently, looking at his watch.

"You don't understand," I said, "it is pure penance to breathe. My head aches. My eyes feel like round razor blades, and it's only a matter of minutes before I go to that big utility room in the sky."

"I feel the same way when I sleep too long in the mornings," he said.

"But it's only six-thirty," I said huskily.

"So, eat a little bacon, hash browns covered with catsup . . . and where are you going?"

You've heard it sisters, now what are we going to do about it?

I propose we initiate federal legislation to make women's colds legal in all of the fifty states to be protected under a new law called: Bombeck's Equal Cold Opportunity Bill.

The bill would provide that women would receive more than fifteen minutes to get over a twenty-four-hour virus.

Under Equal Opportunity, her cold would be granted the right to stay in bed and would be exempt from car pools, kitchen duty, laundry, bowling, and visiting the sick.

Any husband who degrades and taunts his wife's cold with such remarks as "Maybe it was the pot roast," or "You're just bored," or "If it hangs on till spring you'd better see a doctor," or "Get on your feet, you're scaring the children," will be liable to a fine.

Any husband who mentions bacon and hash brown potatoes to a dying woman would be put away for fifty years . . . without benefit of trial.

I would also like to see women protected from well-meaning families when you are flat on your back. There is nothing any worse than to lie there looking as sexy as open garbage and have your family get along beautifully.

As Grandma says, "I've never seen your house so immaculate. The children are doing a fantastic job. You really should get help when you get home." (The implications being exactly what you think they are.)

Or a husband who says, "Don't worry about a thing. Your daughter is an amazing cook. I don't know where she gets it. Last night we had steak, potatoes, and green beans. Tonight, she's going to surprise me."

Or a daughter who chirps, "I love keeping house. Did all the laundry today in an hour. I made the boys clean their own rooms. All you have to do is sit on them."

Or a son who smiles, "Wow, did we have a day. I had the gang over and they didn't have to be quiet like when you're home writing. We really had a blast. We helped Dad clean out your kitchen cabinets."

Just when it sounds as though you could be replaced

by a recording, your small son whispers, "The dog wet on the bedroom carpet, the hamster died, we spilled beets all over the refrigerator, argued all day Monday, and the green beans were so tough we fed them to the meal worms."

You know, I'm going to live with that kid in my old age.

I make old age sound like a certainty. I don't mean to. What with the doctor shortage, you are lucky to get an appointment . . . especially if you're new in town.

"Hello," I said over the phone, "I have just moved into the community and wonder if the doctor could. . . ."

"I'm sorry," interrupted the nurse, "but the doctor does not accept any new patients."

"I'm not really new," I giggled. "I'm forty-four years old. Some of the parts you can't even get any more."

"You do not understand," she said, without glee in her voice. "The doctor does not take on any more patients."

I called the Medical Society in the area and in calling the list of numbers she gave me discovered Dr. Frizbee did not work on weekends . . . or the Friday preceding them; Dr. Coldiron had a phone that was unlisted; Dr Shuxley could not see me until two days before Thanksgiving, unless I was bleeding profusely and in that event could work me in as an emergency sometime the week of October 10; and Dr. Dlux was home with a cold he couldn't seem to shake for the last six weeks.

I became as frustrated as Martha Mitchell facing a telephone strike. The idea of getting a doctor became an obsession with me . . . a game, so to speak.

"Hello there," I said huskily to one doctor. "This is Joey Heatherton. I have a chest cold." (Click)

"Hi there. This is Mrs. Arnold Palmer. If you could see me for five minutes, I could take five strokes off your game." (Click)

"Hi. I wasn't feeling too well and wondered if you

would consider seeing me if I told you I made house calls." (Click)

"Hello. I'm an old, rich person and want to leave my fortune to someone to whom I am grateful and has shown me some kind act." (Click)

"Doctor? Are you wearing your stethoscope? Fine. You're invited to a come-as-you-are party." (Click)

Doctors often work sixty hours a week. The golf on Wednesday is a myth. They are bogged down by paper work and hypochondriacs. Few of them want their sons to walk in their shoes.

But the fact remains, I had to lie to get a doctor to see me. I told him I was well and felt wonderful, but just needed a physical for camp.

When I talked with a doctor about the shortage, he said they could possibly alleviate the shortage by releasing medical students into the community. But the real problem was that so many doctors were specializing, it cut down on the number of general practitioners.

I found this to be quite true when I took my cold to Dr. Weazel last week.

"Is it a summer or winter cold?" he asked.

"Summer."

"Then you'll want to see my colleague, Dr. Stamp, on the third floor."

Dr. Stamp's nurse got out a form and asked, "Where is the location of your summer cold? Head, nose, or chest?"

"Mostly in the nose," I said. "I can't seem to breathe."

"That would be Dr. Alvenaz on the eighth floor."

"Which nostril," said Dr. Alvenaz's nurse.

"Mostly my left."

"That's too bad," she said. "Dr. Flack is out of town. His calls are being handled by a wonderful right-nostril man, Dr. Riggs. He's down on the fifth floor."

Dr. Riggs took a look at my left nostril and said, "Do you sneeze a lot?"

"Oh yes," I said.

"I thought so. We have a great sneeze specialist in the building. Just joined forces with a top fever-blister consultant. They're on the main floor off the lobby. I think perhaps he can help you."

Dr. Hack was quite reticent to infringe on Dr. Flack's left nostril, but he did say he thought he could prescribe a box of nose tissue and a Berlitz record of a German saying, "Gesundheit."

"I could venture one step further," he said, "and suggest two aspirins and bed."

"What kind of bed?" I asked. "Double, rollaway, single, twin, bunk, or trundle."

"It doesn't really matter," he fidgeted.

"And what about the mattress?" I insisted. "Firm, hard, semi-firm, downy soft, or orthopedic?"

"I really don't think. . . ."

"And what about the sheets? Cotton, percale, satin, contour, fitted, patterned, floral, pastel, or white. Let's talk about pillows while I'm here. Should it be duck, down, goose, swan, diseased chicken, what?"

"Really, madam," he said, "I am only a sneeze doctor. Don't make trouble."

How insulting could you be to a doctor whose stethoscope is made out of tinker toys?

Besides, these experiences in a doctor's office are vignettes compared to the drama of a hospital visit.

After every hospital stay, I experience a gnawing sensation that sends giddy tingles up and down my spine.

I have the feeling it is only a matter of time until hospitals go the way of zoos: they will lock up all the visitors and let the patients/or animals roam free.

I base this on a recent experience in the hospital, at

which time there were more tourists roaming around my room than there were in Rome during Easter week.

Just for the record, I made note of the people ministering to my needs:

A fledgling pathology worker who kept thrusting a hypodermic needle into an orange and mumbling to himself, "I think I got the hang of it now."

A farsighted candy-striper who was arranging two rosebuds in a specimen vial.

A visiting clergyman who wanted to pray with me.

A dietitian engaging in an in-depth dialogue with me on why I did not eat the Tomato Surprise.

Three neighbors who were having a heated discussion on who was legally responsible for my expiration if I should fall out of bed.

An intern who was lost.

And an assortment of workers who were specialists in their respective fields: window-sill wiper, under-the-bed duster, sheet smoother, mail deliverer, pillow fluffer, bed-raiser supervisor, water-pitcher captain, boy paper carrier, milk-and-cracker foreman, and pulse-and-temperature recorder.

Any minute I expected to hear Ben Grauer announce that in sixty seconds, the big ball would fall from the New York *Times* Building and it would indeed be another New Year.

The Woodstock atmosphere not only slows down a patient's recovery, it often turns the "sickee" into a totally different personality. I have seen shy, introverted women enter a hospital who were too embarrassed to say the word pregnant (when they were). Two weeks of hospital routine and they were whipping up and down the halls like wood nymphs dressed only in a table napkin and an ID bracelet. (I once discovered myself discussing my irregularity with a TV repairman I had never seen before in my life.)

The very idea of locking up the help and the visitors and letting the patients run the hospital captures my imagination. I get some kind of a thrill just thinking about standing in front of the cage occupied by my night nurse, Mrs. Needles. I would wait until I saw signs of her deep breathing. Then I would rattle the cage vigorously. When that didn't rouse her, I would thrust my flashlight into her face, put my arm inside, grab her by the throat and shout into her exposed ear, "Mrs. Needles! *Mrs. Needles!* Will you need something tonight to help you sleep?"

In my imagination, I have dreamed of an entire section devoted to visiting birds. I know a lot of strange birds who deserve to be visited back.

The Good News Warbler:

She's the gem who sits at your sickbed and informs you that while you are flat on your back your children are under the close scrutiny of the welfare department, your dog wandered off, possibly to die, she hasn't seen your car since they towed it home, and your husband is finding solace with a person who is well. (She will mention how your hair reminds her of Elliott Gould.)

The Long-Winded Mean-Mouth Thrush:

This is the well-meaning visitor who can't make it to the hospital in person, so she calls you on the telephone and talks . . . and talks . . . and talks. There is no way to get her off the line.

"As I was telling Frank just the other day. . . ." she rambles.

"I am having labor pains three minutes apart, Delores," I venture, "I have to hang up now."

"Wait a minute," she says, "did I tell you what Leroy brought home from camp. This'll tear out your stitches."

"The doctor is here now, Delores. He wants to take out something."

"Hang on a minute," she says irritably, covering the

mouthpiece. Later she returns and says, "Leroy is bugging me. He wants to know if he can have a soft drink. I swear all that sugar is going to rot his teeth."

"Can I call you back, Delores?" I ask feebly. "I'm beginning to black out now."

"Well, don't," she commanded, "until I tell you about Bernie's garage sale."

The Bungling Loony Bird:

I can hardly wait to call on this rare species when she's in custody. She's the wrongo who can't do anything right. She never comes to the hospital empty-handed. There's a bag of caramels for the toothless; cookies for the diabetic; pizza for the gall-bladder recoverer; roses for the allergy sufferer, and a book on ice hockey for the new mother.

The AMA Crested Warbler:

Whatever you've got, the AMA Crested Warbler knew someone on a soap opera with the same thing who had to be written out of the script.

A civilian, she is virtually in love with the drama of the hospital and will perch for hours on your bed taking your pulse and quoting from old aspirin bottles.

The Loitering Bedside Hawk:

This is the bird who arrives in time for hospital breakfast and never knows when to go home. She is usually someone you have known for about two weeks. Once you have ascertained you look rotten, you pursue such breathless-making subjects as What outdoor scene are you going to pick for your next checkbook? Does Tom Jones wear lifts in his shoes and should the government control the sale of fireworks?

The Swift-Tailed "Caught Cha":

This is the species that swoops through your door in moments that would at the very least be called "inopportune."

When you are lying flat on your back with your sheet

off, trying to pull your gown over your hipbone, the door will crash open—and it's Caught Cha.

When you have a compact mirror trained on your backside to see if the last shot administered left a crater in your skin, a draft of air will herald the Caught Cha.

The Bluebird of Happiness:

For obvious reasons, I have saved my visit to my doctor until last, as timing is of the essence.

I would visit my doctor only when he is bathing in a saucepan with one arm balancing the soap and washcloth and the other clutching a wet sheet to his body.

Then I would hover over his breakfast tray and with a look of horror point to a mound of white and gasp, "What is that?" Finally, I would fight my way through the crowds of people around his bed and before parting toss a humorous little one-liner over my shoulder like, "Get some rest."

Happy Mother's Day, Colonel Sanders

Looking back, I realized now that I married too young, but when you're forty-three and in love, who can tell you anything?

The transition from typewriter to toilet bowls is never an easy one. I always wondered if someone ran an ad in the New York *Times:* WANTED: Household drudge, 140 hour week, no retirement, no sick leave, no room of own, no Sundays off. Must be good with animals, kids and hamburger. Must share bath, would 42 million women still apply?

Every day my husband returns to his lair and asks mechanically, "What kind of a day did you have today?"

Resentment caused me to turn on him the other day and ask, "What kind of a day did you think I had?"

He grabbed a pencil and began to write. The result was headed:

ERMA'S DAY

8 A.M.: Get everyone out of the house and make a fresh pot of coffee. Leave just enough in pot to spoon out a cup for husband at dinner and a piece to chip off for his breakfast.

8:30 A.M.: Separate husband's socks . . . from one another. Make sure there is not a pair that matches.

9 A.M.: Lint socks. Gathering up small pieces of thread and dust is tedious, but it is worth it to see him bite his necktie in half, out of rage.

10:00 A.M.: Go through his jewelry box and take out all the large cuff links with B on them and put them on your blouses.

10:30 A.M.: Take tucks in all of his underwear and slacks to make him think he is gaining weight.

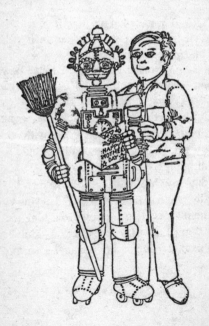

11:00 A.M.: Borrow his razor blades to take the hem out of the living room draperies.

Break for lunch, followed by "As The World Turns."

3 P.M.: Wash good tennis sweater in hot water with red blanket.

4 P.M.: Invite small neighborhood children into the garage to play with husband's power tools.

5 P.M.: Put an onion into the oven to make husband think dinner is on.

6–11 P.M.: Tell husband what a hard day you had.

"Well," he said triumphantly, "did I miss anything?"

"Yes," I said, "when you are asleep, I run out and move the car seat up under the steering wheel so your legs will cramp."

"You know," he said, "the more I think about it, the more I'm convinced that someday women will be replaced by automation."

On that thought I went to bed only to dream that my husband ran away with my modern kitchen and was living in sin with it in an apartment in New Jersey.

"What kind of wife is this?" I asked, storming into his room without knocking.

"The best kind," he said. "When I come home, Phyllis, the electric cocktail stirrer, has a drink for me; Iris, the oven, has hot hors d'oeuvres on her shelf; Evelyn, the broiler, has a steak going; Margaret, the electric percolator, has fresh, hot coffee brewing; Roberta, the stereo, has soft music going; and when I am finished, Bertha, the disposer does away with my leftovers neat and tidy."

"You're not being fair," I sobbed.

"Oh, but I am. Elsa, the dishwasher, never grabs my plate out from under me before I am finished. And Toni, the refrigerator, works day and night to keep me in ice cubes."

"You're pretty cute, aren't you?" I said. "But what about your laundry?"

"Meet the twins, Shirley and Selma. Shirley washes my clothes to perfection. Never have I had to wear pink underwear or use faded peach handkerchiefs. And Selma, God love her, dries my clothes smooth and knows enough to keep her lint trap shut when I am tired."

"What's that dinging?" I asked.

"It's Iris, reminding me my Baked Alaska is ready. Isn't she a treasure?"

"So were the Dead Sea Scrolls," I said dryly.

"You're jealous," he smiled.

"Who me? Ridiculous. I just wondered who is going to warm your feet on a cold winter night and pick up after you?"

"No sweat," he said. "Meet Caroline, my electric blanket, and Jeanine, my electric broom."

"But who listens to your problems and laughs at your jokes?"

"I've got Sophie, a portable tape recorder, and Bunny, a cassette of warm, soft laughter. Really, my dear, you are wasting your time here. What could I possibly have with a real, live wife that my girls cannot do with maddening efficiency?"

I shook him suddenly out of a sound sleep.

"If you wanted a girl with a clock in her navel, why didn't you marry one?" I shouted.

See what I mean? Not for a minute do men appreciate the frustrations . . . the futility . . . the loneliness . . . the decisions we make in a single day.

To begin with, there is no such thing as a simple household chore. All of them have built-in aggravations.

Take the laundry. I wish you would.

My washer is on a new tack.

For years, it has seen fit to eat one sock out of every pair I have fed into it. Oh, I questioned it at first, but after a while everyone adjusted. They would put a cast on one leg, or a bicycle clamp around their trouser cuff or laugh nervously and say, "Good heavens, one sock *is* brown and the other one pale blue, isn't it?"

Three weeks ago, my washer did a reversal. It gave birth to a pair of men's briefs. They did not look familiar to me, but then, I get a little behind sometimes and have been known to stumble onto navel bands in pre-soak. (The baby is thirteen.)

For starters, I put the briefs on my thirteen-year-old's stack of laundry. He came down early the next morning and asked, "Where's a belt? My shorts keep falling down."

"Don't be funny," I said. "Put them in your brother's drawer."

The sixteen-year-old came out the next morning and said, "Where's a belt?"

"Give them to your father," I said dryly.

My husband said, "They aren't mine. They've got elastic in them. I haven't owned a pair with new elastic in years."

I figured out they had to belong to a friend of my son's who had just spent a few weeks with us, so I put them in an envelope and mailed them to Ohio. We received them back within a week with a note attached. "These are wonderful for showing home movies on but somewhere there must be someone walking around who needs them. They aren't ours."

I sent them to my father who also spent a few weeks with us. He called long distance to say if this was his birthday present, would I please exchange them for the right size.

The shorts became an obsession with me. Where did they come from? Where had they been? Was there an anxious mother somewhere looking into her washer and saying, "Is that all there is?"

I asked the milkman if they looked familiar. (He has never gotten out of his truck since. He just sets the milk at the end of the drive.)

As a result of the handling, the briefs became soiled, so yesterday I put them back into the washer. After the spin cycle, I felt around for them and they were gone. In their place, I found a faded beach towel with little black footprints on it that I have never owned in my life.

I'm going to pretend I didn't see it. The headaches are coming back.

My second favorite household chore is ironing. My first being hitting my head on the top bunk bed until I faint.

An ad in a midwest newspaper read, a while back, "WANTED: Women to do ironing for housewife ten years behind in everything. Must have strong courage and sense of humor. Phone———."

I figured there was a woman I could live next door to in perfect harmony. I iron "By appointment only." I learned long ago that if I ironed and hung three dresses in my daughter's closet, she would change three times during dinner.

The other day my son wanted me to iron his jeans for a class play. "Which leg faces the audience?" I asked, with my iron poised in mid-air.

"Boy," he said, "you're sure not Mrs. Breck."

I hadn't thought about Mrs. Breck in years. She was an antiseptic old broad who used to live two houses down from me. She had an annoying habit of putting her ironing board up on Tuesdays and putting it away again at the end of the day. (What can you expect from a woman who ironed belt buckles?)

One afternoon I dropped in on her as she was pressing the tongues in her son's tennis shoes.

"You know what you are, Mrs. Breck?" I asked. "A drudge."

"Oh, I enjoy ironing," she grinned.

"You keep talking like that and someone is going to put you in a home."

"What's so bad about ironing?" she smiled.

"No one does it," I snapped. "Did you ever see the women on soap operas iron? They're just normal, American housewives. But do you ever see them in front of an ironing board? No! They're out having abortions, committing murder, blackmailing their boss, undergoing surgery, having fun! If you weren't chained to this ironing board, you could too be out doing all sorts of exciting things."

"Like what?" she chuckled, pressing the wrinkle out of a pair of sweat socks and folding them neatly.

"You could give Tupperware parties, learn to Scuba dive, learn hotel management while sitting under a hair dryer, sing along with Jack La Lanne, collect antique barbed wire, start chain letters. I don't know, woman, use your imagination!"

I read the newspaper ad again. It intrigued me, so I dialed the number and waited.

"Hello, Mrs. Breck speaking . . ."

Son of a gun. It sure makes you feel good when you had a part in someone's success, doesn't it?

That fact that housewives are a misunderstood group was evident recently at a cocktail party. A living room psychologist was analyzing women who move furniture every time they cleaned house.

"Basically," he announced, "they are women who hate men. They cannot bear the thought of a man entering his home and walking across the floor without cracking his femur bone in three places. Rearranging furniture is a little more subtle than putting a cobra in a basket by the bed."

I took exception to his remarks. "Women who rearrange furniture have imagination. They have creativity. They have style. . . ."

"Don't forget hernias," he prompted. "Why is it a woman cannot pinch the clasp on her bracelet, yet can move a fifteen-hundred-pound freezer from the basement to the garage?"

Everyone laughed, but it occurred to me that men don't really know boredom as women do. If we had offices with secretaries with appointment books you could do our week with one original and six carbons. Same old egg on the plate, same old dustballs, same old rumpled beds, same old one-of-a-color socks in the wash.

An attack of monotony does strange things to a woman. Once, for no reason at all, after I finished cleaning the bathroom, I filled an apothecary jar full of popcorn and put it on the back of the commode.

Another time, I put an early American eagle on the doghouse. Usually when I clean, I will fill a brandy snifter with water and food coloring and float a zinnia in it which goes stagnant in ten minutes and hatches mosquito larvae by nightfall.

I will try anything to break the monotony . . . change a light bulb, paint a wall with an artist's brush, put the dining room furniture in the living room and the living room furniture in storage.

"When I clean tomorrow," I told my husband, "I am going to take out the tub in the bathroom and put the washer and dryer in its place. Then I'm going to cut out the front of the tub and make it into a campy sofa for the living room."

"If you want to change something, why don't you wash the draperies?" he mumbled.

"If you're going to use language like that, the least you could do is send the children out of the room," I said.

Two things have always bothered me about my domesticity. One was when the children sent Colonel Sanders a Mother's Day card, and the other was a remark made by my husband one evening who said, "Get out of the kitchen before you kill someone."

I have always felt cookbooks were fiction and the most beautiful words in the English language were "room service."

My insecurity at entertaining was compounded when I read an item in a social column recently about a bash for several hundred people where the host was quoted as saying, "We had a pig in our freezer and our neighbors had turkeys in theirs, so we just decided to have a turkey and swine party."

I opened my freezer. I had three snowballs left over from last winter, fourteen packages of chicken innards that were being saved until "garbage day," two radio batteries that someone said would recharge themselves if put in the freezer, a half-eaten piece of taffy with a retainer brace in it, and thirty pounds of hamburger.

I could just imagine myself picking up the phone and saying, "Hey gang, wanta come over Sunday? I'm roasting chicken necks in a pit and for dessert we are having fresh batteries over snowballs."

When I entertain, I do it with all the grace of a water buffalo with a migraine. To begin with, a spontaneous, impromptu, instant party takes me anywhere from three to four weeks to pull off.

First, I must amass enough glasses. This involves numerous trips to the gas station.

Then I must make the house look as though it has never been lived in by children. We must paint, plaster, buy pictures, remove the baby gate from the top of the basement stairway (we haven't had a baby in thirteen years), and replace all the dead house plants with fresh green ones.

Finally, I must pull together a menu.

"What should I serve?" I ask my husband, leafing through a stack of cookbooks.

"How about that wonderful pork Mary Lou made on her rotisserie?"

"How about Sloppy Joes?" I ask.

"Hey, I know. The Spanish dish we had at the Dodsons with the whole clams in it."

"How about Sloppy Joes with a lot of pepper?"

"Maybe we could have a luau and serve something from the pit?"

"How about Sloppy Joes buried in the sandbox?"

Our parties go well enough, I guess, but it's a little disconcerting to open up the paper the next day and read where your husband is quoted as saying, "We had 30 pounds of hamburger in our freezer that wasn't moving and our neighbors had 30 bottles of catsup without labels to unload, so we had a Sloppy Joe Party."

Of course, we've never given a party in our lives that something (or someone) didn't crawl inside our wall and die.

It's the price you pay for rustic, rural living.

In my mind, I visualize a group of mice meeting on a cornfield and one of them says to the other, "Bufford, you don't look too good."

"Oh, I'll be all right," says Bufford, "it's just a head cold."

"Nevertheless," says the leader, "why don't you check in at Bombeck's wall?"

The night of our last party, Bufford didn't make it to the wall. He staggered into our old pump organ and died.

My husband came into the house, sank to his knees and gasped, "Not again! Where this time?"

"In the pump organ," I said.

"Can't we get rid of the odor?"

"Only if you want to paint the living room."

"We mustn't panic," he said, patting his wrists with a deodorizer wick. "We're just going to have to make sure that no one plays the organ tonight." We both nodded.

The party was in high gear when Max Marx sat down to play the organ. I grabbed a can of deodorizer and followed him.

"What are you doing?" he asked, annoyed.

I turned the deodorizer on myself. "It's Skinny Dip," I said feebly, "to make me irresistible."

I watched in horror as he pulled out the stops on the organ and started to pump. As the bellows wheezed in and out, spreading misery throughout the house, three women fainted and one man put out his pipe.

"I say," he said, pausing, "do you have a dog?"

"We have three of them, but they're outside."

He began to play again, then stopped and sniffed. "Is someone in the house cooking sauerkraut? Or making sulfer with a junior chemistry set?"

"No."

"Is someone wearing old gym shoes?" he persisted.

His wife came over at that moment and leaned over his shoulder.

"Max, your music stinks!"

"Is that it?" he said, and moved on to the kitchen for a stronger drink.

We Have Measles . . .
It Must Be Christmas

The other day Brucie complained, "My head hurts and my nose is stuffy."

"Ridiculous," I said. "It's too early. Christmas is a whole week away."

Normal people can always predict when the holidays are near at hand. There is an air of excitement, the smell of holly, the ringing of bells, the singing of carols. At our house, if we have measles, it must be Christmas.

Down at the laundromat, I am known as Typhoid Mary.

"What are you having this year for Christmas?" they ask as I sort my clothes.

"Well, I've got one exposure to chicken pox, one who has only had mumps on his left side, and one who just threw up to keep things interesting."

It's never serious enough to be an emotional drag, but I've forgotten what real Christmases are like. I cornered my friend Donna Robust and begged, "Tell me again about Christmas at your house."

"Well," said Donna, "on Christmas morning I get up first and. . . ."

"Start going through the yellow pages to find a drugstore open," I said, my eyes glistening.

"No, no," she laughed. "I turn on all the lights around the Christmas tree. Then I ring the sleigh bells and. . . ."

"I know, I know," I said excitedly, "it's pill time. You give one a spoon of Coke Syrup, another an aspirin, and the baby a suppository for nausea."

She shook her head. "I summon them all around the tree to open up their presents. Then, after breakfast, we all get dressed. . . ."

"Can you imagine that?" I sighed. "Everybody dressed."

"Then we go to church and that afternoon we have fifteen or twenty people in for Christmas dinner."

"Once I saw my dad on Christmas. He slid two batteries under the door for a robot monster that didn't include them. We were contagious at the time."

"I bet that was nice," she said.

"Oh, and another time the doctor dropped by to check on us and brought in a bit of snow on his boots. The kids went wild."

"Maybe this year things will be different," said Donna, patting my hand.

"Maybe so," I sighed. "But tell me again about how you all get dressed and go out. . . ."

The Twelve Days of Christmas

On the first day of Christmas my husband gave to me a car with a dead battery.

On the second day of Christmas my husband gave to

me two suits for pressing, one dog for worming, and a car with a dead battery.

On the third day of Christmas my husband gave to me three names for drawing, fifty cards for sending, one gift for mailing, and a car that would take till Saturday.

On the fourth day of Christmas my husband gave to me one house for trimming, one tree for buying, one broken ladder, and a short trip to surgery.

On the fifth day of Christmas my husband gave to me three kids for shopping, walnuts for chopping, fruitcake for baking (with Mom's recipe), one house for cleaning, eight doorbells, one Avon call, and a paper route for delivery.

On the sixth day of Christmas my husband gave to me one garage attendant, one hostile doorman, two window washers, one errand boy, and three single secretaries.

On the seventh day of Christmas my husband gave to me one instant party, one broken punch bowl, one littered carpet, three pounds of chip dip, and three unemployed secretaries.

On the eighth day of Christmas my husband gave to me a driveway for snowing, red nose for blowing, long list for going, and a stinking home cold remedy.

On the ninth day of Christmas, my husband said to me, "I have a chipped tooth." "Did you get my rented suit?" "Hope you brought enough loot" for the annual Christmas charity.

On the tenth day of Christmas my husband gave to me a pageant by the wee tots, a gift of a flu shot, and a bird that looked better off than me.

On the eleventh day of Christmas my husband gave to me a bike for construction . . . where are the instructions? . . . these are for a wagon . . . my spirit is draggin', and besides it's a quarter past three.

On the twelfth day of Christmas my husband gave to

me gifts of a steam iron, half a water heater, plunger for the bathroom, a blouse size 43, two scented soaps, one paperback, three hair nets, and a toothbrush with a dead battery.

The Newsletter

I regard the family Christmas newsletter with a mixture of nausea and jealousy.

Nausea because I could never abide by anyone organized enough to chronicle a year of activities. Jealous because our family never does anything that I can talk about on a religious holiday.

For years, I have been assaulted with Frieda and Fred's camping adventures, Marcia and Willard's bright children (their three-year-old has a hit record), and Ginny and Jesse's kitchen-table version of "The Night Before Christmas."

"You know something?" I announced at dinner the other night. "We're a pretty exciting family. This year, instead of the traditional Christmas card, why don't we make up a newsletter?"

"What would we say on it?" asked a son.

"What everyone else says. We could put down all the interesting things we did last year. For instance, you kids tell me anything you did in school that was memorable. (Silence) This is no time for modesty. Just spit out any award or recognition you received throughout the school year."

Finally, after five minutes, one son said, "I passed my eye examination."

"See," I said excitedly, "I knew if we just thought about it a bit. Now, where have we been that's exciting?"

"We got lost that Sunday and went by the industrial school where you told us one of your relatives made license plates."

"I don't think our Christmas list wants to read about that," I said. "Let's see, have I been any place?"

"You went to that Sarah Coventry jewelry party last spring."

"How about that?" I said excitedly. "Now, keep it rolling. Anyone got promoted? Married? Divorced? Hospitalized? Retired? Give birth? (Silence)

"Anyone say anything clever last year? How about the year before that? Did anyone compose a song? Write a letter? Belch after dinner? (Silence)

"Anyone protest anything? Stop biting their nails? Scrape a chair in the Christian Science reading room? Get up in the morning before ten? (Silence)

"Anyone lick a stamp? Kick the dog? Wash their gym suit? Sit up straight in class? Replace a light bulb? Breathe in and out?"

They all sat there silently contemplating their year. Finally, I brought out a box of Christmas cards.

"What are you doing? We thought you were going to send out a family newsletter for Christmas."

"No sense antagonizing the poor devils who sit around and do nothing all year."

"Are You Awake?"

I just signed a pact with the kids.

If they will sleep on Christmas morning until 3:30, I promise not to let my head fall in the gravy during dinner as I have done in previous years.

The "Christmasthon" has been a tradition at our house since the children were old enough to walk. They appear in our bedroom at some unreal hour and chant, "Mama."

"What?"

"It's Christmas."

"Christmas who?"

"Christmas morning. Are you awake?"

"No."

"Want me to turn on the light so you can see how late it is?"

"And blind your poor mother on . . . what day is it again?"

"Christmas."

"Tell Daddy. He'll be choked."

"Daddy."

"I gave at the office."

Minutes later, Daddy is out of bed, shouting, "For God's sake, do they have to sit around with a flashlight counting the hairs in my nose?"

Once on our feet, we are literally caught up in the ear-splitting pandemonium that is Christmas.

The numbing boom-boom of padded pajama feet on the carpeted stairway.

The deafening click of the switch as the lights illuminate the tree.

The crash of tissue in eager little hands.

The shattering roar of tongues licking peppermint.

The piercing scratch of the dog who wants outside.

The blatant blast of the fire as it crackles in the hearth.

The resounding clang of cereal detonating itself in a bowl.

What seems like days later my husband says, "You look like Dorian Gray. What time is it?"

"It is 3:15 A.M."

"Time flies when you're having fun," he says, yawning.

"Will you keep it down?" I say irritably.

"Just What I Wanted"

Last year, in Macy's department store in New York, Santa Claus offered his knee to housewives. The results were interesting. As a group, housewives didn't make a lot of demands as to what they wanted so much as what they didn't want. They didn't want drudgery in a box with a ribbon tied around it, any more than their husbands wanted a rubber band organizer for his office.

Our image has become so distorted through television that men are often confused as to what really turns us on.

The other day I was on my hands and knees in the bathroom trying to scrape a piece of caramel off the seat (don't ask!). I was wearing a pair of slacks with the zipper pinned together, a sweat-shirt belonging to my daughter. My hair looked like a $1.98 wig that had been reduced.

My husband peered in with a package under his arm and said, "I didn't know what to buy you for Christmas. You've got everything."

I sat back on my heels numbly.

He had that same look on his face the first Christmas we were married and he bought me a cemetery lot and explained, "I was eating your pot roast and this idea came to me like a flash."

He had that same look on his face the year he gave me an appointment card for a free yearly chest X ray/or 5,000-mile checkup—whichever came first.

He had that same look on his face last Christmas when he bought me a barber's kit so I could cut the boys' hair on the patio and save a few bucks. When I saw it, I ran from the room, crying.

"Well, what did you expect, for crying out loud," he said, "a jewel for your navel?"

"And why not?" I charged.

"I didn't know your size!" he shouted back.

"Just once," I said, "I would like you to look at me and not see a plastic person with sticky jelly on her elbow, oatmeal in her hair, and a diaper pin on her blouse. Once . . . just once . . . I'd like you to see me as I really am—a temptress!"

I felt sneaky, but I had to know what he had in mind for this Christmas. I went quickly to the shelf in his bedroom where he had just put the package. I prayed. Please not a garden hose, a cheese slicer, or a card of iron-on patches. Slowly, I felt inside the box and eased out the contents. It was a large, fake jewel with a note: "One size fits all, Nosey."

The Ayes Have It

For years I've been telling educators they put school levies on the ballot at the wrong time of the year. If they had mothers vote during the Christmas vacation, there isn't a levy in the country that would fail.

There is something about being trapped in the same house for a week with a kid with a bouncing ball that makes education important.

I don't know which is worse—the child with nothing to do or the child with something to do.

The kid with nothing to do wants to talk about it. The $200 worth of Christmas toys are all dependent on four

Size C batteries that are available only at a Japanese discount house in Japan.

They cannot possibly invite anyone in because there would be a group of them with nothing to do.

They cannot go outside because they would meet someone else with nothing to do and be doubly bored.

They cannot do homework, make beds, empty garbage, or dry dishes because a vacation is when you're supposed to have nothing to do.

They cannot watch television because that is something to do when there is nothing else to do.

The kid with something to do drives you nuts because whatever he does it involves you.

"If you could run in and pick up Charlie and Tim and stop at the store on the way back and get some ice cream and chocolate syrup, we could make a mess in the kitchen."

"We're waiting for you to get down the sled that Daddy stored under the lawn furniture, then we'll get out of your hair."

"Could we have three mason jars, the wheels off your vacuum sweeper, a box of cotton, two pieces of foil, and a banana? We got an idea."

As I was telling my neighbor Maxine yesterday, "Kids today have no stimulant for imagination. The dolls eat and belch, toy cars go 70 miles an hour, their planes fly, their rockets launch, their stoves cook, their games light up, and TV takes them all over the world. They're bored."

"You're right," said Maxine. "Whatya wanta do today? Take a nap?"

"I'm getting too old," I said. "Wanta look for loose change in the chairs?"

"That's boring. We did that yesterday. We could hide from the kids."

"Na . . . It's no fun when they're not here."

Clever and Creative

The holiday season brings to the surface a breed of women who is not to be believed.

As a matter of fact, I have spent a lifetime avoiding these congenital savers who appear from nowhere and ask, "You're not throwing away those old corn pads just because they're used, are you?"

Their entire life revolves around making something out of nothing—or is it the other way around?

I was at a luncheon the other afternoon when, heaven forbid, I found myself surrounded by not one, but three Junk Junkies. It was like being in a foreign country.

"Do you need any more popsicle sticks?" asked Dorothy.

"No, dear, but I'm short on piano keys."

"I've got some in my basement," said Karen, "unless you want to use up my Tabasco bottles and the arthritic chicken bones."

"We'll get the favors out of the way, then we'll start collecting glass from the rear windows of cars for our decanters," she said proudly. Then, noticing I was there, she turned to me and asked, "What are you making for Christmas?"

"I am making myself sick."

"No, no, I mean what creative things are you doing this year?"

I thought for a moment. "I am wrapping a bed sheet around the bottom of the Christmas tree to cover up the wooden stand." (There was silence.) "I am using a wet sponge to moisten the stamps before I put them on my Christmas cards." (No one moved.) "I replaced the light in the cellar stairway."

Finally, Dorothy spoke. "You mean to say you haven't

saved your eggshells for Christmas ornaments? Your old apple cores for sachet or your potato peelings for centerpieces?"

"Oh, I saved all of that together," I said.

"What did you make out of it?" they asked excitedly.

"Garbage."

The women looked at me piteously . . . unbelieving. Suddenly, because I felt inadequate and spiteful, I wanted to shock them. "What would you say if I told you I throw out my old coat hangers by the carload?" (They winced.) "And another thing. I don't save my old milk cartons or my bleach bottles." (They gasped.) "And I don't dress my extra toilet tissue in a red suit for Christmas with a cotton beard. What do you think about that?" (They turned from me.)

They will feel more kindly toward me when they hear I paid fifteen dollars for a termite-ridden log painted gold and stuffed with eight hundred jelly beans on coat hangers with paper hats at the Christmas bazaar.

Would You Believe, Love Goddess?

On the occasion of my fortieth birthday, I went into the Bureau of Motor Vehicles to have my driver's license renewed.

The man behind the counter mechanically asked me my name, address, phone number, and finally, occupation.

"I am a housewife," I said.

He paused, his pencil lingering over the blank, looked at me intently and said, "Is that what you want on your license, lady?"

"Would you believe, Love Goddess?" I asked dryly.

If there is one hang-up that plagues every woman it is the "Who am I?" thing. How can we serve a husband, kids, an automatic washer, the Board of Health, and a cat who sits on top of the TV set and looks mad at you because you had her fixed and still have something left over for yourself?

In my lifetime, I have had many identities.

I have been referred to as the "Tuesday pickup with the hole in the muffler," the "10 A.M. standing in the beauty shop who wears Girl Scout anklets," and "the woman who used to work in the same building with the sister-in-law of Jonathan Winters."

Who am I?

I'm the wife of the husband no one wants to swap with.

The whole affair was humiliating.

We went to a neighborhood gathering and noted with some embarrassment and shock that they were wife-swapping. One by one a couple would slip off until finally there was only my husband playing "The World Is Waiting for the Sunrise" on a five-string ukelele and me eating the leftover canapés on everyone's paper plate. We went home without speaking a word to one another.

That night I had a dream in which my husband and

I awoke in a world where everyone had entered a commune . . . and no one wanted us.

The two of us wandered from one group to another begging to join their free society only to be rejected for one reason or another.

At one commune, we almost made it. The leader looked at us closely and said, "In a commune, we all work in various capacities. Some women tend children, others cook, others clean house, others do laundry. In what capacity would you like to work?" she asked, turning to me.

"Do you have any openings for sex objects?" I asked

"Hah!" snarled my husband. "With that line you could get the Nobel prize for humor."

Turning to my husband, the leader asked, "And you, sir, what are some of your talents that would be considered contributions to our group. Chopping wood? Building fires? Harvesting crops?"

"I can play 'The World Is Waiting for the Sunrise' on a five-string ukelele," he said.

"Don't be modest," I interrupted. "He can also watch two hundred televised football games in a single weekend without fainting. He can reseat a commode with Play Doh, and he can make himself invisible when it comes time to take out the garbage."

"We are a sharing society," said the leader in a soft voice.

"Did you hear that, Harlow?" I asked, nudging my husband. "A sharing society. That's not going to be easy for a man who sleeps with his car keys."

"You should talk," he barked. "We were married twelve years before you let me drink out of your Shirley Temple mug."

"Please," said the leader of the commune, holding up her hand in a sign of peace, "I don't think a commune is the place for you two. You are compatibly incompatible."

"Which means?" asked my husband.

"Which means you are too married to live in peace and harmony."

The rest of the dream was a nightmare. We are the last two married squares on the face of earth living in a swinging free-marriage-less society. When we check in at a hotel, bellhops snicker when they see we have luggage. Managers stiffen when we sign our names Mr. and Mrs. and say, "We don't want your kind in our hotel." Our children are taunted by cruel playmates who chant, "My Mommy says Your Mommy and Daddy are living in wedlock. Yeah yeah!"

I awoke suddenly from the dream to the voice of my husband who said, "For crying out loud, what's that car doing parked in our driveway? They're just sitting there looking."

"Well, who do you think they are?" I shouted. "They're tourists from the commune here to look at the married freaks."

I'm the mother of no. 39's football pants. A woman leaned over at the high school football game last week and said, "Hi, aren't you the mother of no. 39's football pants?"

"Yes," I said.

"You don't know me," she said, "but our sons share the same pants. You see, my Boyd sits on the bench while your son sits in the bleachers and the next week Boyd sits in the stands while your son gets to sit on the bench."

"I see," I nodded.

"What kind of bleach do you use for the stains?"

"Just a pre-soak," I said, "and then my regular detergent."

"I thought so," she said. "A few weeks ago, you over-did."

"Weren't the pants clean?" I asked.

"They were too clean, dear. The boys complained. When they're too white it looks like they never play."

"I'll watch it," I said.

"Have you met any of the other mothers yet?"

"No."

"Well, over there is the mother of 71. She has pants all to herself. He's the captain, you know. Beside her is the grandmother of 93's. He got the new stretch ones. They're trying them out. Wonderful woman. Comes to every game. And of course you know the mother of no. 15's pants. She's the quarterback's mother. Her pants take a beating. At the first away game, they were dragged in the mud twenty-three yards before they were finally ripped."

"Well I never," I said.

"Listen, don't worry about the red stains on the left knee this week."

"Blood?" I asked.

"Jelly bun," she said. Then she added, "You know when women like us have so much in common, we ought to get together more often. Why don't you call me, and we can chat over lunch."

"What's your name?" I called after her.

"Alternate bench mother of 39's pants. I'm in the book!"

I'm an illegible name tag. My husband and I are veterans of innumerable school functions (he being in education). That means something like a simple coffee after a flute concert is turned into a ceremony, second only to a national political convention.

Miss Prig is in charge of fashioning small name tags shaped like tulips out of colored construction paper which are pinned to your back. Then Mr. Flap, the football coach, announces that on one side is the name of a famous personality. You are to mingle throughout and by asking questions of each guest find out who you are . . . an ice breaker, so to speak. When the game is finished, you then turn the name tag to the other side, and *voilà!* you know who you are.

Invariably, Miss Toasty, who is in charge of straight pins, blows it, and seventy-five adults are circulating around a room with one arm behind their backs asking painfully, "Am I living? Am I in politics?"

Actually, I question the value of name tags as an aid to future identification. I have approached too many people who have spent the entire evening talking to my left bosom. I always have the insane desire to name the other one. It is most disconcerting. Without ever looking at my face, they will say, "Hello there, so you are Edna Bondeck."

"No," I will say, smiling engagingly at their left bosom, "I am Erma Bombeck."

"Don't tell me," they say. "You are related to that tall man over there with a crick in his right arm from holding the name tag behind him."

"Right," I say, my eyes never leaving their tag for a moment, "and you are Fruit of the Loom."

"No, that's a label from my underwear that got stuck in my name tag while my arm was behind my back. Are you new in the area?"

"Yes I am. And it's wonderful meeting so many new chests . . . er, people."

"I'm sure it is. See you around."

The entire evening is a faceless one. At the end I say good-by to the blonde with the exceptional posture, the braless militant, the chest of hair under the body shirt and kcebmoB lliB.

"Oh, for crying out loud," says my husband. "It's me with my name tag upside down."

I looked carefully into his face. "Oh yeah. Let me see some identification."

I'm Edna. My mother-in-law and I have a great relationship. She calls me Edna and I call her on her birthday, Mother's Day, and Christmas.

At the wedding when she insisted they put a funeral flag on the fender of her car and drove with her lights on, I sensed somehow I was not what she would have chosen for her son.

But, God love her, she has a sense of humor and somehow we have all survived. She has accepted me for what I am. A mistake. And I have learned to live with her through the miracle of sedation.

One of her idiosyncracies, however, I will never adjust to. I call it her Last Breath Performance.

Check this. I am driving the car and she is sitting beside me. Out of the clear blue sky, I hear her suck in her breath, moan slightly and slump, steadying her head with her hand. I wait, but she doesn't exhale.

The first time this happened I figured (a) She was leaving the car on a permanent basis; (b) I had closed the electric windows on a gas-station attendant and was towing him by his fingers; (c) We were being followed by a tornado funnel.

Instinctively, I jammed on the brakes of the car, nearly hurling her through the windshield, turned around, grabbed her by the shoulders, and shouted hysterically, "What's the matter?"

"Darn it," she said, "I just remembered I forgot to lock my back door."

During subsequent drives, I was to learn that she gasped and groaned at girls in shorts, roses in full bloom, a half stick of gum discovered in her raincoat, and the realization that tomorrow was her sister-in-law's birthday.

She didn't limit her Last Breath Performance to the car.

When she watched television or read the newspaper, she would inhale noisily, freeze, put her hand over her mouth, and say, "How do those poor people in Needles, California, stand the heat?"

I pride myself on being able to live in peace with my mother-in-law, and she puts up with me. The other day we were driving together, when she sucked in her breath, clutched her purse, and mumbled, "Oh my!"

Figuring she had just remembered her dental appointment, I kept moving and promptly smacked into a truck pulling out from the alley.

She shook her head and made a clicking noise with her tongue. "I tried to warn you, Edna, but you wouldn't listen."

I'm the dog's mother. As everyone knows I hold the record for the longest post-natal depression period ever. I could hardly wait for the Empty Nest Syndrome at which time I was going to climb in it, eat bourbon balls before breakfast, watch soap operas, and eventually run away with a vacuum cleaner salesman.

On the day the Empty Nest became a reality, I found to my horror there was a dog in it—which the family explained would keep me company. I needed company the way a man reading *Playboy* needed his wife to turn the pages for him.

The dog was friendly enough, had fair manners, and was playful. He only had one hang-up. He had to be let in and out of the house 2,672 times a day.

Some dogs have a blade-of-grass complex. They can't seem to pass one without stopping and making it glisten. This beast never passed a door without scratching it, jumping up to the door handle and howling like he only had two seconds before he would no longer be responsible for what happened.

At the end of the first day I was near exhaustion. I had not gotten the breakfast dishes cleared off the table, the beds made, or the laundry started.

"I'll bet you were playing all day with that dog," teased my husband.

"What makes you think that?" I asked.

"Look at the way that little dickens is jumping up and down."

"He is aiming for your throat. He wants out."

"Don't be ridiculous. He just came in."

Finally, the dog let out a shriek that took off the tops of our heads and threw himself at the door.

Mechanically, I opened up the door and stood there with my hand on the knob.

He gave another yap and I opened up the door and he was in again.

"Why did he want in after you just let him out?" asked my husband.

"Why do fairies dance on the lawn? Why is the Pope always a Catholic? Why indeed?" The dog yipped and I opened the door for him to leave again.

"You mean to tell me it's this way all day?"

I nodded, at the same time opening the door so he could bounce in again.

"I got it," said my husband snapping his fingers. "We'll go out when he goes in and when he comes out we'll go in. That way we'll confuse him into not knowing if he is in or out."

Standing there huddled in the darkness on the cold porch scratching with our paws to get in, I tried to figure where I went wrong. I think it was when my mother said, "Grab him. You're not getting any younger."

I'm room service in tennis shoes. "What in heaven's name is that hanging over your dirty-clothes hamper?" asked Mother. "It looks like a basketball hoop made out of a bent coat hanger."

"It's a basketball hoop made out of a bent coat hanger," I said.

"It looks terrible."

"That's easy for you to say," I said. "You don't have to run through dirty underwear in your bare feet or find the laundry before you can do it. When the boys improve on their hook shots, I'll have it made."

"What's this?" she scowled.

"You mean that bar across the door you just cracked your head on? It's an exercise bar so the boys can build up their muscles."

"And this ironing board," she persisted. "Don't you ever get tired of falling over it? Want me to take it down?"

"What for?" I asked. "We're not moving."

The trouble with Mother is she has forgotten what it is to live in a house furnished in Contemporary Children. I used to fight it too. At one time I was so naïve I thought only edible things belonged in the refrigerator, bicycles without wheels should be discarded, and if you had eight people to dinner, all the glasses had to match.

I went crazy trying to keep an antiseptic house in a wet shoestring world. Then one day I was doing cafeteria duty with a mother of six children who said a curious thing. "I wonder how my kids will remember me. Will they remember me as a Mother who never had rings around the bathtub or will they remember the popcorn we ate in the living room?

"Will they remember how many committees I chaired, or will they remember the fresh doughnuts in the kitchen after school?

"Will they remember how cleverly I co-ordinated the blue in the sofa cushions with the pillows or will they remember I hung the outline of their hand in the living room like it was an original Renoir?

"It's funny," she said, "I came from a large family and I can't even remember what color my bedroom was or if there was mud in the hallway or fingerprints around the light switches. All I can remember is the laughter, the love, and a crazy basketball hoop my mother made out of bent coat hangers and put over the clothes hamper and how my mother was always there to talk to."

Well, I can't begin to tell you how that story brought tears to my eyes. I wanted to be that kind of mother.

Yesterday, I stacked my cookies in pyramids and waited for the kids to come home from school. The phone rang. "Mom? I went home on Greg's bus. We're going to shoot baskets and mess around."

"But . . . when are you coming home?" I asked soulfully.

"I don't know. His brother will bring me."

"Wanta know what I did today?" I asked excitedly.

"Not now, Mom. You can tell me when I get there."

"But I'll forget it by then."

"Write it down." (Click)

I ate a cookie and watched the clock. The door opened and I greeted our daughter.

"Hi, guess what I got on sale today?" I said, following her to her bedroom.

"Tell me while I change," she said.

"Change for what? You going out again?"

"I'm going to the library. They're holding a couple of books I have to pick up today."

"Don't you have time for milk and cookies and talk with a mother who is always here?"

"I'm on a diet. You eat 'em, but don't ruin your dinner."

"It's no fun eating by yourself. Can I go with you?"

"You'd be out of place in the library. No adults go there in the afternoon."

I ate another cookie and awaited the arrival of my other son.

"Did I get any mail?" he asked.

"A thing that looks like a picture from Baltimore. Did I tell you the funny thing the butcher said today?"

"Hey, that's Jim O'Brien's autograph I sent for. I'm gonna call Brian. Why don't you run along and watch TV."

I sat there deflated. That's the trouble with mothers today. No wonder we're rotten. There's no one to communicate with us. No one to share our day after school. No one to give us a sense of importance. Small wonder we hang around the beauty shops in gangs, join organizations, have long lunches with fattening desserts. There's no one to care. I stood outside of the bathroom door and called in to my son. "I forgot to tell you something. Are you in there?"

"Who is it?" he asked.

"It's Mother."

"Mother who?"

I'm a household word. A neighbor of mine suggested that since I have been writing a column for the newspaper, I have become a household word.

"You mean like bleach, leftovers, and grease-clogged sinks?"

"Of course not," she said. "I mean like Flip Wilson, Carol Burnett, and Martha Mitchell."

"Oh really now," I said, "you do run on. If you asked someone what a Bombeck was, they'd think it was a nearly extinct bird in the Everglades who eats mosquito eggs."

"My dear, you are wrong," she insisted, "you have quite a following."

With some immodesty, I decided to test her theory one afternoon when I called home from an airport in Philadelphia.

"Hello, operator. This is Erma Bombeck calling. I'm a household word and. . . ."

"Is Household the party's first name or last?" she asked.

"Neither, I was being funny. This is Erma Bombeck and I. . . ."

"Steinbeck?"

"No, Bombeck. That's B as in Boy O-M-B-E-C-K."

"Mary Household Bondack. Do you have an area code?"

"No, I don't want to talk to Mary Household Bondack."

"Then you wish to call station-to-station. If you do not

know the number in that city, you may hang up and call the area operator and 555-1212."

"Operator. Don't hang up! OPERATOR! (redial) Operator, I wish to call collect to . . . my name is Erma Bombeck. Not Ernie. Erma, E as in Edna r-m-a Bombeck."

"Bomberg? Bromfield? Brombreck? Brickbat? Would you spell that again, Miss Beckbomb?"

"Look, you're pretty warm with Brombeck. Let's ride with that one. I am trying to call home collect and this is my number."

The operator speaks. "I have a collect call from Mrs. Edna Brombecker."

My son answers. "That's my mom and she isn't home now. She is in Philadelphia."

"Dear heart," I yelled, "it's Mama. Accept the charges."

"My mama isn't home now. Can I take a message?"

"Yeah," I shouted. "Call *Mrs.* Erma Bombeck at. . . ."

"How do you spell the last name?" he asked slowly.

I hung up and sat there awhile, numb. I can't believe this is how Martha Mitchell made it as a household word.

Joan of Arc? A friend confided to me the other day that whenever an unpleasant situation arises, she resorts to play-acting. She pretends she is a character living out a scene.

"You are some kind of nut," I said.

"We all do it," she replied. "I've seen you when your husband goes out of town for a few days. I don't know who you are, but you're certainly not yourself."

She was right, of course. Actually, I am several characters when my husband goes out of town. As I stand in the driveway, clutching my shawl and drawing my children close to me to stave off the harsh winds, I am

Marmee March, the brave young mother in *Little Women*. Upon my frail shoulders rests the responsibility of the family. I play it to the hilt. "Prithee have a good trip," I yell. Then to the children, "Come, let us go in and pop corn and sing 'Rock of Ages.' "

By the second day, being alone with the kids, I am not so gallant. I am Stella Dallas who is cast aside by society to serve and suffer without friends, family, or love. I am forgotten by the world (Mother didn't even call) and sentenced to a life of loneliness, pain, and "Let's Make a Deal."

By the third day, as I visualize that bum living it up in a Holiday Inn Motel, I go into my Belle Watling routine. She's the woman of pleasure in *Gone With the Wind*. I tell myself I was just a passing diversion to bear his three children, but now he has abandoned me and gone on to brighter lights in tinsel town. Is it my imagination? Or did I really get the cold shoulder at the meat counter?

My St. Joan is probably my best effort. I perform it my fourth day alone. It's a consumptive performance where I clomp around in my robe and slippers until noon and when the washer repairman says, "I found a pair of training pants in your pump. That's thirty-four dollars," I just cough and say, "It doesn't matter any more, really."

By the fifth day, the kids have me on the run and they know it. Discipline and reasoning are gone. Play-acting has lost its fascination. As my husband pulls into the driveway, I approach him with a band of plastic daisies around my head while I shred my apron into small pieces.

"Who are you today?" he asks.

"Ophelia," I snap.

"That bad?" he asks.

"That bad."

But Seriously, Folks . . .

Time.

Time.

It hangs heavy for the bored, eludes the busy, flies by for the young, and runs out for the aged.

Time.

We talk about it as though it's a manufactured commodity that some can afford, others can't; some can reproduce, others waste.

We crave it. We curse it. We kill it. We abuse it. Is it a friend? Or an enemy? I suspect we know very little about it. To know it at all and its potential, perhaps we should view it through a child's eyes.

"When I was young, Daddy was going to throw me up in the air and catch me and I would giggle until I couldn't giggle any more, but he had to change the furnace filter and there wasn't time."

"When I was young, Mama was going to read me a story and I was going to turn the pages and pretend I could read, but she had to wax the bathroom and there wasn't time."

When I was young, Daddy was going to come to school and watch me in a play. I was the fourth Wise Man (in case one of the three got sick), but he had an appointment to have his car tuned up and it took longer than he thought and there was no time."

"When I was young, Grandma and Granddad were going to come for Christmas to see the expression on my face when I got my first bike, but Grandma didn't know who she could get to feed the dogs and Granddad didn't like the cold weather, and besides, they didn't have the time."

"When I was young, Mama was going to listen to me read my essay on 'What I Want to Be When I Grow Up,' but she was in the middle of the 'Monday Night Movie' and Gregory Peck was always one of her favorites and there wasn't time."

"When I was older, Dad and I were going fishing one weekend, just the two of us, and we were going to pitch a tent and fry fish with the heads on them like they do in the flashlight ads, but at the last minute he had to fertilize the grass and there wasn't time."

"When I was older, the whole family was always going to pose together for our Christmas card, but my brother had ball practice, my sister had her hair up, Dad was watching the Colts, and Mom had to wax the bathroom. There wasn't time."

"When I grew up and left home to be married, I was going to sit down with Mom and Dad and tell them I loved them and I would miss them. But Hank (he's my best man and a real clown) was honking the horn in front of the house, so there wasn't time."

"I've Always Loved You Best"

It is normal for children to want assurance that they are loved. I have always admired women who can reach out to pat their children and not have them flinch.

Feeling more comfortable on paper, I wrote the following to put on the pages of their baby books.

To the Firstborn

I've always loved you best because you were our first miracle. You were the genesis of a marriage, the fulfillment of young love, the promise of our infinity.

You sustained us through the hamburger years. The first apartment furnished in Early Poverty . . . our first mode of transportation (1955 feet) . . . the seven-inch TV set we paid on for thirty-six months.

You wore new, had unused grandparents, and had more clothes than a Barbie doll. You were the "original model" for unsure parents trying to work the bugs out. You got the strained lamb, open pins, and three-hour naps.

You were the beginning.

To the Middle Child

I've always loved you best because you drew a dumb spot in the family and it made you stronger for it.

You cried less, had more patience, wore faded, and never in your life did anything "first," but it only made you more special. You are the one we relaxed with and realized a dog could kiss you and you wouldn't get sick. You could cross a street by yourself long before you were old enough to get married, and the world wouldn't come to an end if you went to bed with dirty feet.

You were the child of our busy, ambitious years. Without you we would never have survived the job changes, the house we couldn't afford, and the tedium and the routine that is marriage.

You were the continuance.

To the Baby

I've always loved you best because endings are generally sad and you are such joy. You readily accepted the milk-stained bibs. The lower bunk. The cracked baseball bat. The baby book, barren but for a recipe for graham cracker pie crust that someone jammed between the pages.

You are the one we held onto so tightly. For you see, you are the link with a past that gives a reason to tomorrow. You darken our hair, quicken out steps, square our shoulders, restore our vision, and give us humor that security, maturity, and endurity can't give us.

When your hairline takes on the shape of Lake Erie and your children tower over you, you will still be "The Baby."

You were the culmination.

The Lost Christmas

There is nothing sadder in this world than to awake Christmas morning and not be a child.

Not to feel the cold on your bare feet as you rush to the Christmas tree in the living room. Not to have your eyes sparkle at the wonderment of discovery. Not to rip the ribbons off the shiny boxes with such abandon.

What happened?

When did the cold, bare feet give way to reason and a pair of sensible bedroom slippers? When did the sparkle and the wonderment give way to the depression of a long day? When did a box with a shiny ribbon mean an item on the "charge"?

A child of Christmas doesn't have to be a toddler or a teen. A child of Christmas is anyone who believes that Kings have birthdays.

The Christmases you loved so well are gone. What happened?

Maybe they diminished the year you decided to have your Christmas cards printed to send to 1,500 of your "closest friends and dearest obligations." You got too busy to sign your own name.

Maybe it was the year you discovered the traditional Christmas tree was a fire hazard and the needles had to be vacuumed every three hours and you traded its holiday aroma for a silver one that revolved, changed colors, played "Silent Night" and snowed on itself.

Or the year it got to be too much trouble to sit around the table and put popcorn and cranberries on a string. Possibly you lost your childhood the year you solved your gift problems neatly and coldly with a checkbook.

Think about it. It might have been the year you were too rushed to bake and resorted to slice-and-bake with no nonsense. Who needs a bowl to clean—or lick?

Most likely it was the year you were so efficient in paying back all of your party obligations. A wonderful little caterer did it for you at three dollars per person.

Children of Christmas are givers. That's what the day is for. They give thanks, love, gratitude, joy, and themselves to one another.

It doesn't necessarily mean you have to have children around a tree. It's rather like lighting a candle you've been saving, caroling when your feet are cold, building a fire in a clean grate, grinding tinsel deep into the rug, licking frosting off a beater, giving something you made yourself.

It's laughter, being with people you like, and at some time falling to your knees and saying, "Thank you for coming to my birthday party."

How sad indeed to awake on Christmas and not be a child.

Time, self-pity, apathy, bitterness, and exhaustion can

take the Christmas out of the child, but you cannot take the child out of Christmas.

I Love You, Edith Bunker

Bigots may be all right in their places, but would you want your daughter to marry one?

Edith Bunker did the day she said, "I do, I will, and I'll keep doing it until I get it right" to Archie Bunker, the Irish Godfather of TV's "All in the Family."

Personally, I love Edith Bunker. She hasn't read anything current since a cereal box offered an African violet to people with irregularities. She regards the six o'clock news as a filler between "As the World Turns" and "Roller Derby." She fills up her husband's plate at picnics and apologizes because the baked beans oozed over his chicken. If Gloria Steinem asked her to make a contribution to her sex she'd say, "Honey, Archie gives at the plant."

What's to envy about Edith? She's a giver and God knows there are few of them left in the world. Edith is at the end of every line, whether it be at the bank, the check-out, or the clinic. She would drive Archie to the hospital for a paper cut. But she would refuse anesthetic for her own surgery if it cost extra. She would hang a picture over her living room sofa that the milkman's wife painted by number.

She would lend you her new Christmas sweater and wouldn't complain if you sweat in it. She is one of the last of the vanishing breed of listeners—remember them? They are people who sit quietly and look at you in the face when you talk and when you're finished there is a silence. They haven't been thinking of a story they could tell.

Edith has a tolerance toward humanity and unconsciously looks for the bright side. She would find humor in Jane Fonda's acceptance speech for the Oscar.

Actually, Edith is not too complex. What you see is what she is. Edith has never learned about the plastic veneer or sophistication that people cover themselves with. If it were suggested to her that she not refer to Phase II as a bar of soap, she'd say, "Am I pronouncing it wrong?"

It is a sad commentary on my life, but I don't know many Edith Bunkers. The people I know still wear dark glasses indoors even though they fall over things. They refuse to have people in for dinner until all their dishes match. They are bored, miserable, depressed, and unfulfilled because in 1965 Betty Friedan told them they were. (Would Betty lie?)

I have a theory if anything is ever to be resolved with mankind it won't be the Archie Bunkers with the wall-to-wall mouth who will do it. And it probably won't be Meathead and his wife Gloria (who put the IN in "All in the Family"). It will be the Edith Bunkers. Their unselfishness, their regard for human feelings, their patience, their caring, and their love of everyone will bring it about.

Flag

On television the other week a group of students were talking about their confrontation with New York construction workers. "We made a mistake," said one of the students. "We attacked their symbol—their flag. We shouldn't have done that. It's important to them."

The phrase stuck in my mind. *"Their* flag. *Their* symbol." I thought it was theirs too. Or is it? As a parent, I guess I always thought respect for the flag was congenital. Is it possible I was so busy teaching the basics, I never took the time to teach "flag."

"Oh say can you see by the dawn's early light. . . ."

(Don't slouch. Pick up your feet. Don't talk with food in your mouth. Stop squinting. Turn that radio down. Get off the phone. Tie that shoestring before you trip on it.")

"Shoot if you must this old gray head but spare your country's flag. . . ."

("Don't snap your gum. Stop eating all that junk before dinner. Sit up straight. Look at me when I talk to you. Your eyes are going to stay crossed someday. Get your homework done. Wear boots.")

"I pledge allegiance to the flag of the United States of America. . . ."

("Shut that door behind you. Get the mud off your shoes. Quit rustling that bag. Go to sleep. Don't slam the door. Leave your sweater on. Get a haircut.")

"If anyone attempts to haul down the American flag, shoot him on the spot."

("Stop fidgeting. Keep your feet on the floor where they belong. Don't talk back. What do you say to the nice lady? Wash your hands. You're letting in flies. Pick up that mess.")

"We came in peace for all mankind."

("You're going to be late. Eat something. Bring me the change. Hang that up. Brush your teeth. Apologize. Get your elbows off that table. Got a clean handkerchief? Tuck your shirt in. Be home early.")

Did I forget to tell them it was their flag they hoisted over Mount Suribachi? Their flag that flies over champions at the Olympics? Their flag that draped the coffin of John F. Kennedy? Their flag that was planted in the windless atmosphere of the moon? It's pride. It's love. It's goose bumps. It's tears. It's determination. It's a torch that is passed from one generation to another.

I defy you to look at it and tell me you feel nothing.

X-Rated World

I got some flack on a column I once did on horror movies. Some readers felt I was condoning violence and bad taste for letting my youngsters see them.

There was a time when I probably would have agreed with them. That's when the world had a GP rating and horror movies were rated X.

Maybe it's time we stopped flapping about the world of make-believe ("Did Tarzan marry the girl or not? And was the chimp illegitimate?") and zero in on the big problem: reality.

We are shocked when our children see rats, snakes, and frogs devouring humans. We can turn our backs when they are live-ins in most slums around the country.

We scream censorship when there is murder committed before our children's eyes on the tube. We can endure it when it appears on the six o'clock news with a dateline: Vietnam.

My children in their short span on earth have seen Watts in flames, mothers with clubs and rocks protesting schools, college students slain by national guardsmen, mass slaughter in California, and political conventions that defy anything they have seen on a movie screen.

They have heard language from congressmen that curls their hair. They have seen animals slain to extinction by humans with clubs and shot at from moving cars. They have flinched from gunshots that fell leaders of countries because they hold views that are different from those who slew them.

I challenge you to protect a generation from violence that has seen the horrors of Kent, Dallas, and Attica.

If it doesn't, it should bother someone that our children are short on laughter. We are giving birth to the most educated, bright, intelligent, serious, dedicated group of adults who ever sat in a playpen. Where is the little mouse who used to outsmart the cat in the cartoons? Where is the newspaperman who used to dress in a phone booth and wear wrinkled underwear with a cape? Where indeed?

Bonnie and Clyde was a joke to young movie-goers . . . a gas. So was *Butch Cassidy and the Sundance Kid.* So was *Willard.* To them, the violence was exaggerated, absurd, unreal.

It's the reality that frightens them and gives them nightmares. God help us. It does me too.